A USEABLE PAST?

Belief, Worship and Song in Reformation Context

Three lectures commissioned by the Chalmers Trust to mark the 450th anniversary of the Scottish Reformation

IAN HAZLETT, DOUG GAY, DOUGLAS GALBRAITH

Edited by
JAMES C. STEWART

CHURCH SERVICE SOCIETY

First published in 2013 by
The Church Service Society, Edinburgh
www.churchservicesociety.org
info@churchservicesociety.org

ISBN 978 0 9927725 0 5

Cover design: Caleb Rutherford.
The window featured is in St Giles' Cathedral, Edinburgh, by James Ballantine and Sons, and depicts the assassination in Linlithgow of the first Earl of Moray. The panel is of his funeral, with John Knox shown as preaching. The inscription reads: 'In memory of Regent Murray by George Stuart Fourteenth Earl of Moray 1881'.

This publication was made possible with the aid of a generous award from the
DRUMMOND TRUST
3 Pitt Terrace, Stirling FK8 2EY

The Church Service Society acknowledge the generosity of
THE STRATHMARTINE TRUST
2 Kinburn Place, St Andrews KY16 9DT
in the making of this book

Typeset by Waverley Typesetters, Warham
Manufactured in Great Britain by Berforts Information Press, Stevenage

Contents

The Contributors

Ian Hazlett

The Revd W. Ian P. Hazlett, DD, is a graduate of Queen's University Belfast, St Andrews and Münster. Formerly Professor of Ecclesiastical History in Glasgow University and Principal of Trinity College, he is now Honorary Professorial Research Fellow at the University of Glasgow. His research work and publication have been devoted mainly to various aspects of the Reformation era in different countries including Scotland, with a particular focus on eucharistic history and text-critical editing, e.g. writings of Martin Bucer, Reformed confessions of faith etc. He is editor of the international journal, *Reformation & Renaissance Review*. He is an elder in the High Kirk of Glasgow, and was sometime member of the Panel on Doctrine.

Email: ian.hazlett@glasgow.ac.uk

Doug Gay

The Revd Dr Doug Gay is Principal of Trinity College Glasgow and Lecturer in Practical Theology at the University of Glasgow. He studied modern history and international politics at St Andrews and divinity at Glasgow. His PhD thesis (Edinburgh) was on ecclesiology and social vision in twentieth-century Scotland. Current research focuses on political theology (including nationalism) and on ecclesiology, particularly issues relating to 'emerging church', and he has published widely in these and related fields. Dr Gay is a minister of the Church of Scotland (for a time similarly serving the United Reformed Church in east London). He was an early practitioner in the field of alternative worship and continues to pursue an interest in contemporary liturgy, preaching and hymn-writing.

Email: doug.gay@glasgow.ac.uk

Douglas Galbraith

The Revd Dr Douglas Galbraith studied arts and divinity at the University of St Andrews and music at the University of Glasgow. Following parish ministry in Scotland, he was appointed Professor of Ministry and Mission, Trinity Theological College, Brisbane. On return, he served as University Chaplain at St Andrews, then as co-ordinator for worship and doctrine, Church of Scotland. During that time, he pursued doctoral studies in church music and theology at Bangor University, North Wales. Now retired, he teaches in the International Centre for Sacred Music, Bangor University, and contributes to similar courses in Canterbury Christ Church University. He is Precentor of the General Assembly of the Church of Scotland, and a member of the Royal School of Church Music's Advisory Panel. He edits the *Church of Scotland Year Book*.

Email: d.galbraith@bangor.ac.uk

James C. Stewart

The Revd James C. Stewart graduated in history and divinity at St Andrews, and holds a Master's degree from Union Theological Seminary in New York. His ministry was spent entirely in Scottish parishes; and, during his time in the Kirk of St Nicholas, Aberdeen, he was for a period Secretary of the General Assembly's Committee on Public Worship and Aids to Devotion. Among retirement occupations he has, since 2002, edited *The Record* of the Church Service Society, of which society he had been President from 1997 to 1999.

Email: study@jascstewart.co.uk

Preface

The three lectures in this volume were commissioned by the Trustees of the Chalmers Lectureship to mark the 450th anniversary of the Scottish Reformation.

The Chalmers Lectureship was founded in 1880 by Robert Macfie of Airds and Oban, a supporter of the principles of the Free Church, with the purpose of upholding 'the Headship of Christ over His Church and its independent spiritual jurisdiction'. After the Presbyterian unions of 1900 and 1929, Macfie's original intention was broadened to embrace 'the general doctrine of the Church and kingdom of Christ, or any subject cognate thereto'. It is an expectation that the Lectures will be published.

The Church Service Society, which was founded in 1865, exists to study and foster interest in the history of the forms and practice of worship, especially in the Scottish Reformed tradition, and to provide material for the aid of current leaders

Robert McFie (1812–99), of Airds and Oban, the founder of the Chalmers Lectureship.

and practitioners in worship. The Society was pleased when the lecturers suggested or agreed that it might publish the lectures.

The first lecture (in the order in which they are printed) may not seem to deal with the Society's main field of interest; but, as Professor Hazlett has pointed out, the Church's worship and song arise out of her belief – and that has been notably the case in our tradition. That his lecture falls within the terms of the Trust goes without saying.

The Society gratefully acknowledges the generosity of the Drummond Trust and of The Strathmartine Trust towards this publication; and the Editor is much indebted to Douglas Galbraith, the Secretary of the Society, for undertaking many of the practical arrangements.

James C. Stewart

The Chalmers Lectures commemorate Rev Dr Thomas Chalmers (d. 1847), preacher, theologian, social reformer and a key figure in the Free Church after the Disruption of 1843.

Reproduced from a printed copy of silhouette by August Edouart in New College, Edinburgh

VESTURES OF THE FAITH

Three Scottish Confessions, 1560–1616[1]

IAN HAZLETT

> For, as it is noted by one of the [Church] fathers, while Christ's coat indeed had no seam, the Church's vesture was of divers colours; whereupon he saith, *In veste varietas sit, scissura non sit* [There is diversity in the garment, but no tear].
>
> Francis Bacon, *Essays: Religious Meditations* (1612): 'Of Unity in Religion', alluding to St Augustine's sermon on Psalm 45:14[2]

Introduction

In 1986, the General Assembly of the Church of Scotland announced that 'although the Westminster Confession retains its status [as the binding subordinate standard of doctrine] ... [the Church] no longer affirmed certain parts', indeed 'dissociated itself from certain clauses'.[3] These relate to aspersions on the papacy, monasticism, the Mass and inter-faith marriage. Such an obviously politic, corporate exercise of a dissenting option is consistent with the qualified liberty of opinion permitted by Articles V and VIII of the Church's constitution (Declaratory Articles, 1921). As is known, the latter were intended primarily for hesitant individuals subject to compulsory subscription.

The provision was the consequence of some robust criticism during the previous forty years in Scottish presbyterian churches of the Confession's stance (actual or alleged) on some fundamental doctrines said to be conscience-binding. There are no grounds for considering this outcome as a legitimation of cherry-picking or accommodation to sub-orthodox theologies. Nor is it approximately equivalent to the notion of strict mental reservation in non-canonical Roman Catholic tradition, although it might equate to 'dispensation'. It is probably no worse than omitting certain verses from hymns or national anthems on the grounds of modern offensiveness or repugnance. Anyway, reading the text of the Westminster Confession (1646) in its entirety reveals that even its authors did not regard their formulations as definitive, indispensable, immutable, infallible or inerrant. This accorded with the relativist, foundational principle of the Reformed confessional tradition ('in light of Scripture this is how we here see things at present') – hence its rich diversity. The 1986 General Assembly reconfirmed this when it stated that the Westminster Confession was 'open to challenge on the basis of further study of Scripture'.[4]

In 1992, the General Assembly issued a creedal update: 'A Statement of the Christian Faith'. However, on the Church's official website, elements of that are paraphrased in such a manner as to state that

> [our] standards of belief are to be found in the Old and New Testament (the Bible) and in the Church's historic Confession of Faith. For a brief summary of our beliefs, it is useful to look at the Apostles' Creed.[5]

Since these two sentences appear under the heading of 'The Apostles' Creed', the 'Church' here refers to the Church Catholic, and the 'historic Confession of Faith' refers to the *Apostolicum*. It is notable that the Creed is then immediately relativised as something 'useful to look at'. I am not sure what the Creed's editors or the Apostles might think about that. Yet it is curious that, while the Church of Scotland's website doctrinal resumé is comfortable in viewing the eighth-century form of the Apostles' Creed as historic (code for 'of historical interest'), it is reluctant to declare the seventeenth-century Westminster Confession, which is much less universal, as historic in that sense too. Yet this would not deny its usefulness either. However, what is the use of a symbol that is no longer part of education for the ministry or of church members of any age or of anyone else, and therefore so subordinate as to be effectively out of the frame altogether? It is true that, from the beginning, the Church of Scotland supplied supplements of 'the-confession-made-easier' kind, such as 'Craig's Catechism', the Small and Large Catechisms and *The Sum of Saving Knowledge*. Since in time these also were seen as hard to handle by learners and teachers (including catechising ministers, even in the seventeenth century), they were gradually discarded with nothing to replace them. The Westminster Confession has ultimately become a somewhat indecipherable memorial monument of doctrine for the Church of Scotland, hallowed chiefly by the 'Constitution' and the Revolution Settlement (1690).

In 2010, a former Principal Clerk of the General Assembly listed six issues of pressing importance for the Church. One of these is the 'status' of the Westminster Confession. He remarks that, while this

> remains our Principal Subordinate Standard after Scripture … [w]e came very close in 1974 to redefining the Confession as an Historic Statement of the Reformed Faith, yet twice within the last four years attempts to revisit the matter have been rejected by the General Assembly.[6]

This is not the place to speculate about reasons for this. In passing, however, one might recall that, paradoxically, the Church of Scotland in the post-1560 era of confessionalisation had fewer scruples about reformulating its doctrines or adopting new confessions, and leaving a trail of historic testimonies. There is nothing erratic in such a policy, as a previous Chalmers Lecturer agreed more than 100 years ago, adding that some early Free

The Confeſſione of the fayht and
doctrin beleued and profeſſed by the
Proteſtantes of the Realme of Scot=
land exhibited to the eſtates of the
ſam in parliament and by thare
publict votes authoriſed as a
doctrin grounded vpon
the infallable wourd
of God.

Matth. 24.

And this glaid tydinges of the king=
dom shalbe preached throught the hole
world for a witneſs to all nations and
then shall the end cum.

Imprinted at Edinburgh,
be Robert Lekprewik.

Cum priuilegio.
1561.

Facsimile of the Title Page of the 1561 edition of the Scots Confession.

From the 1960 Saint Andrew Press edition of the Confession

Church divines were not averse to the notion of limited revision and reconstruction of elements in the Westminster Confession.[7] The modern tradition of formally glossing the confession rather than dispensing with it (or deleting some clauses) was initiated by the United Presbyterian Church in 1877. Two characteristic parameters of a degree of latitude were specified – 'liberty of opinion', but not on 'the substance of the faith' – and adopting the usage of 'faith' rather than the conventional 'doctrine'. This process was advanced by the Free Church of Scotland in 1892 and endorsed for the Church of Scotland in 1921, becoming a *sine qua non* of Church reunion in 1929.

In the eighty-seven years after 1560, the Church of Scotland accepted four different confessions, in 1560, 1581, 1616 and 1647 – something without parallel in other particular Churches over the same period. In addition, a few other Continental confessions were specially commended early on for use in Scotland, such as the Second Helvetic Confession and the Heidelberg Catechism. In the wider Reformed association of Churches in the same era, about sixty-six confessional statements of various kinds were issued. Moreover, the adoption of the Westminster Confession by the Scottish Church in 1647 was subject to qualifications and provisos in respect of church government and relations with the civil authority. As indicated above, however, during the 365 years since the adoption of that Confession, the only tangible institutional movement, sometimes anguished, has been to reaffirm the Confession's essential core teaching, while allowing reservations on less or non-essential aspects, as well as to disown some of its rebarbative statements (if not all). Since 1877, the standard, slightly casuistic technique of adjustment was therefore to make 'declaratory' statements and amend the formulas of questions and subscription. Consequently, the Westminster Confession remains immovable on its plinth. What is said to be 'subordinate' has near-canonical status legally and psychologically, even if only in respect of qualified, formal self-identification – 'yes, but'.

Subsequent discussion here will be historical in the sense of trying to retrieve some of those basic impulses and perspectives of pre-Westminster generations that conditioned their statements, and to untie them from their formulaic straitjackets. There is some value in this. Christianity is not just a religion of feeling, spirituality, lifestyle, altruism, stories and nominal beliefs. It is hitched inseparably to a constitutive historical continuum of faith anchored in salvation history, the communion of the saints, and eschatology, but also to secular historical circumstances and cultures, as in the sense of Augustine's 'double city'. This is hard enough to justify to our general modern culture of blindness to both history and transcendence – not helped by the high-altitude, flight-from-history school of dogmatic theologians influential in much of the past century. There will also be a few remarks on the confessions' dissemination and transmission up to the present.

In connection with anniversary celebrations of the Scottish Reformation (2010) and of Calvin (2009), the Edinburgh theologian, David Fergusson, aptly remarked:

> At a time of rapid change and secularisation, we need to be recalled to our rich heritage lest we assume that the future is one in which we must forget the past, tear up the script and start all over again.[8]

Accordingly, while the pre-Westminster Scottish confessions have obviously long been 'history', they still might have a residual usefulness in the sense at least of recalling where the Church of Scotland came from. Relegation to history does not have to mean despatching to cellars of oblivion or the ivory towers of academia. In circumstances wholly alien to and more immediately threatening than ours, they did aspire to coherence and universality, and strove to exhibit Christian truths, however roughly cast in straitened circumstances. For all their contingent markings, one can acknowledge that the underlying concerns, motivations and spirit of the authors, if not all their utterances, have relevance to congenital human quandaries. Vast expansions in human knowledge, in the understanding of history, in biblical studies and doctrinal criticism in the interim may qualify, but do not negate that. In looking at those faith symbols, one can learn not only about the mentality of the authors but also something about ourselves, possibly.

Why Aberdeen?

The Chalmers Lectureship permits its lectures to be delivered anywhere in Scotland. Traditionally, they have been confined to the Central Belt, and the only notable exception I am aware of is the set delivered at Aberdeen by the Church historian, G. D. Henderson, in 1954. Apart from my own previous location in the city, various other factors contributed to my choice of it as a venue. For example, in 1569 the entire teaching staff of Aberdeen's King's College was dismissed for declining to subscribe to the Scots Confession. This is a reminder that, although tradition speaks of the 'Scots Confession' (not its own title), it was never the confession of all Scots.

Further – and ironically – the reawakening of modern consciousness (in Scotland) of that Confession was also associated with Aberdeen. After the sixteenth, and certainly after the seventeenth century, the Scots Confession largely fell into oblivion. It did come to public notice again in the nineteenth century, firstly through Edward Irving, who published an edition of it, and secondly through John Macleod Campbell, who appealed to its apparent lack of the idea of limited atonement. Since both Irving and Campbell were expelled from the Church of Scotland as heretics, their appeal to the Scots Confession may not have enhanced its reputation among the guardians of orthodoxy. Thus vaguely compromised, it was buried again. It was at Aberdeen in 1937–8 that it was resurrected, by Karl Barth's Gifford Lectures. It's not for me to wonder if Karl Barth as well is in any way heterodox – but it is striking that, in recent centuries, the Scots Confession's appeal has not so much been to hotly conservative or traditionalist theologians, as to frontiers-advancing, creative ones like Irving, Macleod Campbell and Barth.

When Barth started his Aberdeen lectures, many Scots were embarrassed that copies of the Confession were hard to come by. Moreover, in 1937 a German churchman, Theodor Hesse, published in Zurich a useful critical edition of a rare copy of the first edition of the Confession published in 1561. Hesse's edition with introduction and notes in German was not easily accessible or useable in Scotland. One should recall, by the way, that both Barth and Hesse were part of the German Confessing Church that had a special interest in the Confession's putative resistance theory. Later in 1937, and at the short-notice request of the Church of Scotland Publications Committee, the Aberdeen Church history professor, G. D. Henderson, published handy editions with a helpful introduction of the early texts, vernacular and Latin, of the Confession as well as of the Confession of 1581.[9] These have been the versions used and reproduced in one form or other thereafter, superseded now by my own recent, text-critical editions of both in a new series of Reformed confessions being published in Germany.[10]

A final reason for seeking an Aberdeen venue was that I thought it would be a good opportunity to draw attention to one of the best-kept secrets of Scottish church history, namely what is called the New or Aberdeen Confession. This was authorised by the General Assembly of 1616 in the city, at a time when episcopacy was ascendant in the Kirk. The Assembly authorised what may be characterised as an updated and more judicious confession of faith, but subsequently tainted in presbyterian eyes due to that Assembly's episcopalian and royal associations of the wrong kind. This caused one of the few historians who have reported anything on the confession, C. G. McCrie, to remark with irony during his Chalmers Lectures in 1907:

> Could anything good come out of the packed prelatic Assembly of Aberdeen? Well, worse things have emanated from that city of anti-covenanting doctors than the Confession of 1616.[11]

The Three Confessions

Turning now to the three confessions, remarks will focus selectively on the circumstances of their composition, their essential form and nature, impact and significance. One thing to note about them all is that the pithy titles by which we know them are not the original ones. The titles we use are shorthand. The 1560 Confession was never known in Scotland as the 'Scots Confession' until the nineteenth century – possibly derived from the Continental practice of referring to it as the *Confessio Scotica* or *Scoticana*, due to Latin versions that were used abroad. In Reformation Scotland, it was always referred to by the initial words of its title, 'The Confession of Faith'. Once the Westminster Confession superseded it in 1647, it was referred to as the 'Old Confession'. As for the Confession of 1581, its designations have been multiple and are a quagmire of confusion for the unwary. In modern times, only two, mercifully, are in vogue, and reflect ecumenical balance. These are the 'Negative Confession', derived from a contemporary Catholic source, and the 'King's Confession', a title that was favoured by Protestants, episcopalian or presbyterian. However, I have counted thirteen other variations, many used in that era, such as, confusingly, the 'Confession of Faith' and 'The Covenant'. The 1581 Confession's own title was: 'Ane Short and General Confession of the True Christian Faith'. And then there is the 1616 Aberdeen Confession; the General Assembly minutes refer to it as the 'New Confession of Faith'. And King James, who encouraged the undertaking, called it 'A True and Simple Confession of Faith'.

The Confession of Faith, 1560

To state its aims and content in brief: it provides the religious and theological rationale for departing from most of the traditional forms of faith, practice and Church structures, seen as perverted

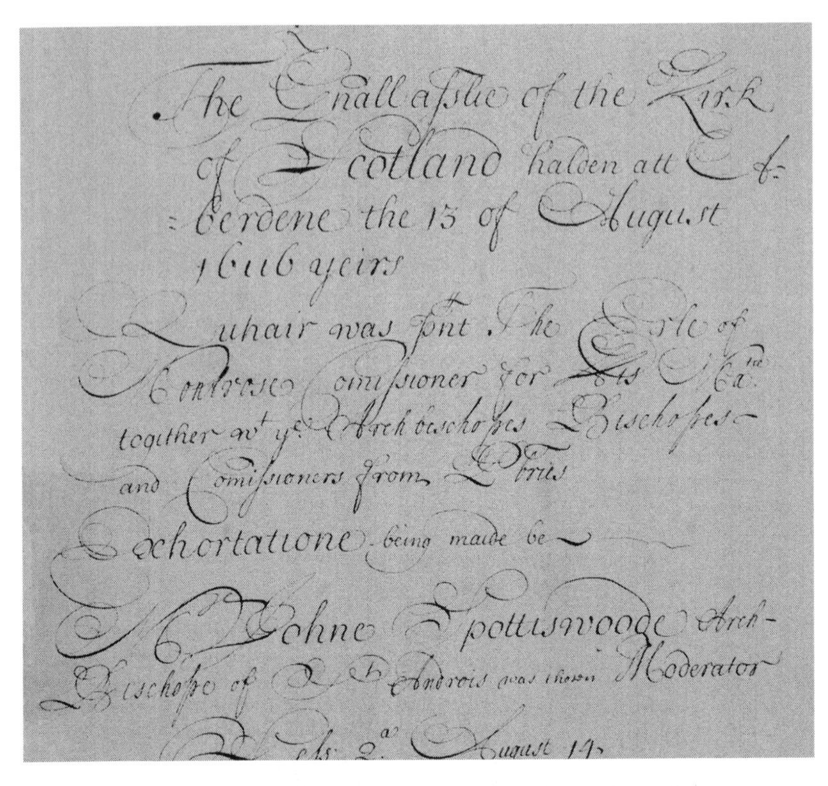
The Generall assemblie of the Kirk
of Scotland halden att Ab-
=erdene the 13 of August
1616 yeirs
Quhair was pnt The Erle of
Montrose Commissioner for his Ma:tie
together wt ye Archbischopes Bischopes
and Commissioners from Pbries
Exhortatione being maide be
Mr Johne Spottiswoode Arch-
Bischope of St Androis was chosen Moderator
Sess 2a August 14

Detail from a late-seventeenth-century transcription of the older of two surviving manuscript records of the 1616 Aberdeen General Assembly; both are in Glasgow University Library.

THE TEXT: The Generall assemblie of the Kirk of Scotland halden att Aberdene the 13 of August 1616 yeirs Quhair was present The Erle of Montrose Commissioner for His Majestie together with the Archbishopes Bishopes and Commissioners from Presbyteries

Exhortatione being maide be [Patrick Forbes, Laird of Corse] M[aste]r John Spottiswoode Archbishope of St Androis was chosen Moderator

Reproduced with permission of Glasgow University Library Special Collections, call-number: MS Gen 1132, f. 465

and dilapidated due to ineradicable human transplants, infection and impurity – or, in its own vocabulary, 'idolatry'. This decadent 'false religion' of bondage grounded in superstition and human vanity will bring damnation rather than salvation. Instead, salvation is wholly extrinsic, has an exclusively divine source: the direct Word of God in Scripture. This demands unencumbered worship of God. It requires instruction in divine doctrine in the framework of the authentic Church of Christ stripped of all deleterious human traditions and accretions, that is, false doctrines and practices. With this liberation theology, Scotland will become a Christian Israel, as it were, a nation of righteousness devoted to proper worship and the honour of God, and so less subject to destructive divine 'judgement' not just at the end of time, but also here and now.

This, then, is a special feature of the Scots Confession, less manifest in other Reformation confessions – namely, it offers a blunt choice between true and false religion, eternal life and irrevocable death of a living kind. On the whole, it is not, therefore, a dispassionate theological exposition, nor does it resemble the rational theologising of the Westminster Confession. The key tones of the Scots Confession, far removed from the conventional, bleak stereotypes of Scottish Calvinism, are inspirational and a *joie de vivre* of religious freedom, if for (some) modern tastes verging on arrogance and browbeating. The immediate task was – as its Preface says – to persuade waverers, who were the large majority in the country. One should hesitate to call such a dimension 'evangelical', partly because the word 'gospel' only appears once in the twenty-five articles, and partly because the notion of forgiveness of sins, essential to the gospel, only explicitly appears in passing in the final article as a kind of afterthought. Instead, one might call its challenging dimension 'prophetic' in a biblical sense, but rather more, as it offers a stark, existential choice between two ultimate destinies – that of eternally blissful communion with Christ, or that of endless burning alive as associates of the Devil.

Some other observations help to explain the confession's distinctive character as a matter of life and death. First: it was precipitously composed. The hour of dramatic Reformation breakthrough in Scotland had arrived in 1559–60 due to a favourable convergence of national and international religious, political and diplomatic circumstances – for example, the decease of the Regent, Mary of Guise, and the disengagement of the military French (Catholic) presence in Scotland, encouraged by the influence of Protestant England under Elizabeth. Lay pro-Reformation leaders in Scotland decided to act quickly and seek secular judicial authority to abolish the old Church before the new Catholic monarch, Mary, arrived from France. This was a bold and revolutionary undertaking. It helps to explain why the Confession of Faith and Reformation legislation by the 1560 Parliament was not legally validated until 1567, after Mary's deposition. The call to submit a confession to Parliament (the English and 'magisterial Reformation' model) seems to have originated from Elizabeth's government, and late in the day. This caught the Scottish Reformers unawares. For, since the spring of 1560, John Knox and his colleagues had been drafting a Book of Discipline on Church restructuring in anticipation of presenting that to Parliament. In addition, while Knox seems to have also envisaged a confession of faith at some point, it was not primarily with submission to Parliament in mind. It was undoubtedly then a bit of a shock when the Scottish Reformers were given only three days' notice to draft a confession for the civil authority.

Secondly: the authors, the six Johns. While all were, in modern parlance, ex-Roman Catholic clerics and had been abroad, just three of them had a public, pro-Protestant Reformation past, namely Knox, Willock and Spottiswoode. Of the other three, Row had been a canon lawyer in Italy until recently, and Winram and Douglas were university scholastic theologians at St Andrews. Winram in fact had been a leading inquisitor in Scotland for twenty-five years, participating in the trial of the martyred George Wishart (1546) and others. Winram had had a good professional knowledge of Reformation ideas. What gave him and Douglas some credibility to advanced Reformation advocates was that, up to 1559, they (particularly Winram) had participated constructively in the abortive, conservative reform initiatives in the existing Scottish Church associated with Archbishop John Hamilton and national Church councils.

The composition of this panel leads to a third point. While the somewhat unbalanced nature of the confession is largely due to the very short time its authors had to frame it, it also reflects their contrasting approaches. The overall style is a peculiar mixture of effervescent biblicism, systematic exposition, high rhetoric, polemical and flowery language. One detects some incompatibility between the Humanist and systematic theological skills of Winram and Douglas on the one hand, and the militantly inspirational, prophetic, declamatory, pugnacious, high-register style of Knox on the other. Furthermore, writing theology in the vernacular was an innovation, not natural or easy for people whose language of education and academic communication was Latin. The exercise was experimental, necessary for the Parliament of non-theologians, mostly unfamiliar with Latin, which would adjudicate the matter. Directness and forcefulness was at a premium.

The presentational issue has a bearing on a fourth observation. It used to be believed that Parliament accepted the confession just as the committee of six had drafted it. But no, it was revised by a parliamentary sub-committee beforehand. This consisted of a leading government figure, William Maitland of Lethington – a man hostile to the idea of church autonomy and to theocratic tendencies – and Winram, who was also a member of parliament by virtue of an Augustinian priorship he held. Information about this procedure comes from a letter of the English ambassador, Randolph, to Elizabeth's secretary of state, William Cecil. The two issues addressed were the strong language that should be toned down, and the statements on civil obedience and disobedience. The un-Calvinist notion of mandatory active resistance to a 'tyrannical' (i.e. committed Roman Catholic) monarch was obviously close to Knox's heart – but whatever had been said originally about permissible disobedience was now excised. Discussions must have been difficult, for what the Confession ends up with are two or three contrasting doctrines in different places. The first reflects that of unqualified obedience to authority in the sense of Romans 13. The second reflects the qualified view typical of Christian tradition – obedience to the civil power is mandatory as long as that power commands nothing contrary to God's Law. A third is deducible from one of the list of good works required by Christians, namely to 'repress tyranny'. That was what grabbed the attention of Karl Barth and the Confessing Churchmen in Nazi Germany.

A fifth point is on the relationship of the Confession to other Reformation confessions. They differed from each other in style and presentation, but not in evangelical substance. All reaffirm in their own words constitutive Christian doctrines as drawn from the Bible and epitomised in the early Church creeds. The Confession does this in the first eleven articles, although with covenantal undertones and implicit repudiation of distinctively Roman Catholic understanding of some central beliefs – for example, original sin, the sacrifice and mediatorship of Christ, (in)certitude of faith, the headship of the Church and so on. After that, the major focus is on the more obviously controverted topics of the day, such as justification, sanctification, ecclesiology, Scripture and tradition, the sacraments (solely the Lord's Supper), Church councils, the role of the civil authority in religion and so on. Calvin's influence is identifiable, but it is neither exclusive nor actually always authentic.

Next, while regional or national churches had their own confessions, they also acknowledged and availed themselves of each other's. There emerged a Reformed corpus or family of confessions, all seen as useful but provisional, and so open to correction and amendment based on Scripture – a matter stressed

Item, It is ſtatute and ordained, that in all time hereafter, the Holy Communion be celebrated in all Kirks within this Realme, at the times following, *viz.* in *B*urrow Townes, the Communion ſhall be celebrat four times in the year, and twice in the year in Landwart Kirks; ſo that one of the times, as well in Burgh, as in Landwart, ſhall be at the terme of Eaſter yearly: And if any Perſon ſhall not Communicat once in the year, at any of the foreſaid times, that it be humbly required of his *Maj.* that the

penaltie

Controversial Act of the 1616 Aberdeen General Assembly requiring the celebration of Communion on Easter Sunday as well as participation in Communion at least once a year. Detail from first printed version of the Assembly minutes, published (1678) in David Calderwood's *True History of the Kirk of Scotland* (the 'short' History), p. 663.

Reproduced with permission of Glasgow University Library, shelf-mark: Special Collections, Trinity College Library, f. 87

by the preface to the Scots Confession: 'If any man will note in this our confession any article or opinion repugnant to God's holy Word, we ask that it would please him of his gentleness and for the sake of Christian charity to admonish us of the same on writing'. There already existed a Scottish tradition for this attitude of interim confession. George Wishart's posthumously published (1548) English translation of the first Helvetic Confession (1536) also added the postscript of the Confession's chief author, Henry Bullinger, found in the original manuscript that Wishart had seen in Zurich:

> It is not our mind to prescribe a certain rule of the faith to all churches and congregations, for we know no other rule of faith but the Holy Scripture. And we are well contented with them that agree with these things, howbeit they use another manner of speaking or confession ... we make it free for all men to use their own sort of speaking ... and we shall use the same liberty ... It was our pleasure to use these words *at the present time*, that we might declare our opinion in our religion.[12]

In Scotland, the Confession had official status in church and state (from 1567). It was the theological and legal basis for abolishing the Mass and papal authority in Scotland. This was all that the 1560 Reformation Parliament did. The 1560 text was formally superseded by the Westminster Confession in 1647, but then restored de facto in 1660 when episcopacy became statutory in the Church of Scotland, and finally abandoned in 1690. Generally, the 1560 Confession does not seem to have been widely disseminated or read much in Scotland beyond the portals of institutions. Unlike the 1581 Negative (or King's) Confession, its text was not included in the National Covenant of 1638, although it is referred to. The *Book of Common Order* did not include it, preferring the short confession of the Genevan English Church, as well as the Apostles' Creed, knowledge of which was required in availing of the two sacraments. Unlike the *Book of Common Order* and Calvin's Catechism, the Scots Confession was never translated into Scottish Gaelic. In addition, in 1566 the General Assembly also approved, adopted and urged the dissemination of the most prestigious of all Reformed confessions, the Second Helvetic Confession penned by Henry Bullinger in Zurich. In Scottish university theology faculties, it was this confession and the Heidelberg Catechism (1563) which were actually studied. The latter was encouraged by King James, who found its balance and moderate Calvinism very palatable.

Lastly, the translation of the Confession into other languages is of interest. The Confession's preface also addresses 'Europe' and 'the world', and the General Assembly urged a speedy translation into Latin for the benefit of people abroad. This did not happen until 1572, done by Patrick Adamson, later archbishop of St Andrews. It cannot have been well marketed, for when in 1612 the Genevans put together a Latin anthology of Reformed confessions, they did their own translation of the Scots Confession. Hence there are two different Latin versions of the Confession. In modern times, there have been various other translations – four different German versions, one French and one Italian.

What about modern English, bearing in mind that the language of the Confession, if not quite 'Scots' (except spelling), is a transitional Scottish English? In 1949, W. C. Dickinson included the Confession in his edition of Knox's *History*. It is not the literal original, now not easily readable for most people, but is made more user-friendly by modernising the spelling and the punctuation. In 1960, the Church of Scotland reissued G. D. Henderson's 1937 edition of the Confession, this time accompanied with an updated English rendering by James Bulloch. Bulloch takes things further than Dickinson, changing some archaic or obsolescent vocabulary and expressions and so on. While his adaptation was serviceable, it is still conservative and traditional. There are also errors and omissions – but, to be fair to Bulloch, he states that he, too, was given very short notice. This version has been the one widely used ever since in various collections. As an experiment, I produced in 2010 (see bibliography below) a completely new English version to make the text more comprehensible to contemporary readers who also may not be very familiar with either biblical or arcane theological terms. Another motivation was that I argue that the 1560 Confession was one of the 100 objects that helped shape Scottish history.

The Confession of 1581

This is the Negative Confession, or 'King's Confession' – since it was issued as a sort of royal proclamation from Holyrood Palace with the force of law, signed by thirty-nine top people in government, including the 15-year-old King James. Only two ministers were among the signatories, one being the reputed author, the ex-Dominican, John Craig, Edinburgh minister and royal chaplain. It arose out of anxiety about surviving loyalty to pre-Reformation faith and practice in Scotland among pockets of the population and some gentry; anxiety about crypto-Roman Catholics in the royal court and in government, such as the Setons of Dunfermline, but especially Esmé Stuart, the king's French cousin, now Duke of Lennox, who then suddenly and prudentially converted to the Reformed Church; anxiety about the counter-Reformation and rumoured invasion plans of powers hostile to the Reformation such as France or Spain; and lastly, anxiety about plots to restore Mary to the Scottish throne and so on. While the general aim was to purge the nation of surviving, old-Church religious sympathies and activities, the immediate aim was to warn closet Roman Catholics in high places that their hopes of securing papal dispensation for being false Protestants were unfounded – instead, they should convert genuinely. And national defence (fear of fifth-columnists) was tied to the issue. In short, twenty-one years after 1560, the Scottish Reformation was still fragile. There had been a deficit of mission and evangelisation (or at least a lukewarm response), and it is no accident that the Confession's publication was accompanied by the more positive and generally serviceable 'Craig's Catechism'.

The 1581 Confession is abnormal as a confession, as it is largely an ad hoc catalogue of about fifty specifically Roman Catholic doctrines and practices that are rejected and banned – everything from purgatory and invocation of the saints to making the sign of the cross and recourse to holy wells. In the looming era of heightening religious conflict and wars in Britain and the Continent, this confession became the identity badge of Scottish Protestantism. After 1581, when people referred to 'The Confession', this was the one they meant. As mentioned above, it formed the first part of the National Covenant in 1638. Since the 1638 document was widely circulated in the British Isles and abroad, its preamble in the form of the 1581 Confession projected the lasting image of Scottish religion. The more judicious might point out that it is actually an appendix or codicil to the 1560 Confession, so that there is a two-part Scottish Confession – but this was a rather academic point in the unceasingly turbulent climate. For all that, the Negative Confession was in one respect an advance on the articles of the Scots Confession – it mentions the 'gospel' three times.

People since the mid-nineteenth century have mostly seen the 1581 Confession as an embarrassing, self-indicting, 'fierce' statement of anti-Roman Catholic prejudice, a manifesto of sectarianism, and have therefore ignored or disowned it. When the Scots Confession was republished by the Church of Scotland in 1960, the 1581 Confession was excluded, presumably in deference to Vatican II. The only modernised edition of it after Henderson's edition of the original in 1937 is the one in recent Yale volumes of creeds and confessions by Pelikan and Hotchkiss – so, it is easily accessible again and there for all to see. The document is not in fact a violent, abusive, bigoted, ultra-Protestant war cry – rather a list of Roman Catholic teachings, customs and usages that are rejected by the Reformed Church, albeit in fairly robust language, some of which is no less moderate than that in the decrees of the Council of Trent. Such rebarbative touches may not be nice, but it was not a crime. Rather than gnash their teeth over this, modern people could ponder on what in various respects was a transparent symptom of two seemingly incompatible concepts of religion and Christianity, bearing in mind that, even for many modern Christians, neither of these concepts may have much relevance any longer. In respect of polemical, militant, Christian self-expression, however, one can certainly hope, as G D. Henderson put it in 1937, that 'we shall not pass that way again'.[13]

At the time, there were some pungent responses to the 1581 Confession from defenders of the old Church. They were banned, but have survived. They were quick to point out that the Confession lacked Bible quotations or references, liberally compensating for the deficit in their own critiques. An eventual major refutation of it was an erudite book of 300 pages published in France in 1601 by the exiled Roman Catholic bishop of Dunblane, William Chisholm III. It included the original Confession and his own accurate Latin translation. This book was soon translated into French in 1604 and validated by the Sorbonne. Church historians of all hues have not devoted any study to Chisholm's book. This is a pity, as hearing the other side could shed more light on the substantive issues.

In the early-seventeenth century, the 1581 Confession came to the attention of all religious parties abroad, initiated by Chisholm's book. James VI's accession to the English throne in 1603 was a headline in international affairs, political and religious. It also provided fodder for psychological warfare and disinformation. Despite his moderate Calvinism, James's irenical attitudes were projected by many Roman Catholics at home and abroad as a sure sign that he was on the path to Rome. However, in that same year (1603), the 1581 King's Confession was published and circulated in London, but without the consent of James, who did not like its 'detestations' by this time, according to reports from the Hampton Court Conference in London. This republication conveyed the opposite message: the new English monarch is a Protestant champion. This was taken up by various avant-garde Protestant interests abroad, so that, by 1604, three further translations were available – a doctored French one by La Rochelle Huguenots, a Dutch one in Amsterdam and a German one in Zurich, all seen as provocative in their respective contexts. And, in 1612, the Genevans did a Latin translation. In short, unlike the 1560 Confession, the 1581 Confession later provoked wide debate arising out of its employment as a banner of combat in the era of increasingly belligerent religious confrontation.

The Aberdeen Confession, 1616

In almost all historiography, old and modern, including episcopalian authors, this interesting item rarely gets more than a passing mention. There is a brief analysis of it within one of the Chalmers Lectures by McCrie in 1906. It belongs to the domain of the lost history of Scottish religious thought. One nineteenth-century writer referred to it as 'an old neglected stone pillar, on which there can still be read, inscribed in clear characters, the faith then professed'.[14]

The main facts about the circumstances of its appearance are these. After James's church policy increasingly undermined the autonomy of presbyteries and the principle of ministerial parity, first by encouraging 'constant moderators' and appointing ministers to some bishoprics (as at Aberdeen in 1600), and then by restoring canonical episcopacy in 1610,[15] there was a strategy to reform the Scottish Church comprehensively. This involved plans for a new, English-style liturgy, a book of canons, a new catechism and a new confession – all part of a coherent vision by the monarch of the three kingdoms aspiring to enhanced uniformity among the Churches of England, Ireland and Scotland. Although James had subscribed the existing Scottish confessions on several occasions earlier in life, he wished to move things on and have a more presentable and up-to-date one drafted. Anyway, he had objected to the way in which many presbyterians were dubiously using elements of the 1581 confession against episcopacy – something that some of the emerging Covenant theologians tended to do as well. For example, the confession's condemnation of 'the wicked hierarchy' (of the Pope) was interpreted by many (controversially) as equivalent to rejection of episcopacy per se.

A General Assembly was convoked by the King in 1616 to meet in Aberdeen. At this assembly, the plan was to set these royal ecclesiastical plans in motion, and hand in hand

The late-medieval choir of St Nicholas (then known as the New Kirk and later as the East Church) where the General Assembly of 1616 was held. From the *Book of Bon-Accord* (1839).

with harsher anti-Roman Catholic proposals. There was concern about 'the defection and falling away from the true religion in this kingdom', as stated in the Assembly's minutes. The Assembly was a largely episcopalian affair. As David Calderwood's *History* noted, delegates turned up in silks and satins, addressing each other as 'My Lord', 'Your Grace', 'Learned Doctor' and so on. However, there were also elected commissioners from presbyteries.

As for the 'Simple Confession of Faith' or 'Articles of Religion'[16] that was submitted and approved: reputedly it had been drafted a few years earlier by two Edinburgh ministers, John Adamson, later Principal (1623–51) of the new 'Toun College' or university in Edinburgh, and John Hall, a constant moderator or quasi-bishop of Edinburgh Presbytery.[17] The early draft is said to have been submitted to and approved by the archbishops of Glasgow and St Andrews, John Spottiswoode and George Gladstanes. That can only have been a formality, as neither of these archbishops had any exceptional theological competence. It came then to the Aberdeen Assembly in August 1616 as a proposal, approved on principle, but then remitted for revision to a subcommittee on the liturgy and catechism

Seal of Archbishop Spottiswoode, on the cover of his *History of the Church of Scotland* (edn of 1847–51).

INSCRIPTION: Sigillum R D Iohannes Archiepiscopi Sancti Andreae [= Seal of the Reverend Lord John Archbishop of St Andrews].

Reproduced with permission of Glasgow University Library, Special Collections: shelf-mark, BC9.y4

due to meet at Edinburgh in December before publication. This was after the north-east's maverick chief warlord and religious dissembler, George Gordon, Marquis of Huntly, was called in and invited to subscribe it. This he did, according to witnesses, without reading it – a familiar practice. Among members nominated for the revision committee were the said John Hall, the Laird of Corse (Patrick Forbes) and the most eminent Scottish religious writer of the day, the covenant theologian, Robert Howie of St Andrews. And then it vanishes from the screen. Further research should explain its fate – but a clue may be in the remark of the much later archbishop of Glasgow, Gilbert Burnet, that the only lawful confession in Scotland was the one of 1560. This has a modern resonance when one considers the Westminster Confession today.

The confession is very succinct and clear. It is a distillation of the best in the 1560 and 1581 confessions. It is singularly positive, affirmative but not pugnaciously assertive. There is no mention of the papacy or the Church of Rome, although here and there some Roman Catholic tenets are explicitly dismissed, but without vehemence. The text is straightforward and calm, the style of the new generation. Although it consists of about fifty-three unnumbered short sections, it is about a quarter of the length of the Scots Confession. It is said that James wanted something restrained like the English Thirty-nine Articles. It must be stressed that there is no compromise on Reformation theology. On the contrary, some key features of Reformation doctrine inadequately dealt with in the Scots Confession are more clearly articulated in the new confession, notably justification by faith, particularly its key elements of imputed righteousness and the inherent continuance of sin. In 1560, the justification doctrine just appeared briefly within the final article. There is also an increased emphasis on effective (but not inherent) righteousness verging on the controversial: humanity is not saved by good works, but in justification they are necessary, they are 'the way to the Kingdom of God' and confirm election. Furthermore, the new confession aligned itself with current trends in Reformed orthodoxy. Chief of these is the inclusion of double predestination by eternal divine decree. In the 1560 Confession, that notion only appeared by implication – either because Knox was resisted on the matter, or because Calvin was known to be reluctant to have it openly preached or presented as a creedal article.

To put the insertion of double predestination into wider context: in the 1590s, Archbishop Whitgift in England had proposed a similar amendment to the Thirty-nine Articles – this was the Lambeth Articles. It failed, as the Queen fell out with him over procedure. And in 1615, the Irish Articles of Religion directed by Archbishop James Usher adopted the double-decree theory. Further, soon afterwards in 1618–19, the international Reformed Synod of Dort in Holland, with Church of England delegates present, was famously to adopt the doctrine in its canons. It was a dogmatic prophylactic. Bearing in mind that the only thing 'damned' in the Aberdeen Confession is an all-too-positive evaluation of the human will, this concern reflects alarm bells about symptoms of relapse into semi-Pelagian or, in the new jargon, 'Arminian', ideas in some Reformed theological circles. The ultimate anxiety about these was that they would facilitate the re-entry of medieval scholastic doctrine on the will and its implications, namely: diminishing the extent of original sin, the Reformation linchpin of justification *sola fide* would be undermined.

All this is very ironic. The Aberdeen Confession, tainted and so airbrushed out in evolving presbyterian Scotland because of its episcopalian and royal associations, was one of various international symptoms of the sharpening of high Calvinist and Reformed orthodoxy. Yet there is no obvious evidence of any subsequent, self-consciously Scottish Calvinist appealing to it.

Conclusion

This look at Scotland's first three historic Reformation confessions shows that, while there was effective consensus on core doctrines, there was considerable diversity of form and expression – explicable by pressing circumstances and critical instability. Yet that which soon caused them to become redundant, or at best 'historic', was the issue of church order. The increasing numbers who believed that presbyterian polity not only belonged to the essence of the Church but was also authorised by divine right, and so the will of God mediated by Scripture, were compelled to advance this construction into the sphere of necessary beliefs and faith statements. That is the real deal-breaker which determined the acceptance of the emended Scottish version of the Westminster Confession. That apart, and allowing for a world radically different from ours today, it is nonetheless confounding that, among all Scottish confessions up to 1647/1690, the spurned Aberdeen one was the sole one that both emanated from and was critically assessed by a church court, a general assembly. All the others came to the Church from without its courts (as seen through modern lenses of practice and procedure).

Notes

1. Edited and moderately expanded version of a Chalmers Lecture (2010) hosted by the Presbytery of Aberdeen in the Church Centre of Midstocket Parish Church on 21 January 2011. Special thanks are due to the Revd George and the Revd Marion Cowie
2. Cf. David K. Weiser, 'Bacon's borrowed imagery', *The Review of English Studies* 38 (1987), pp. 315–24 [here: 321].
3. Its preface to the text of the Westminster Confession on the Church of Scotland website: http://www.churchofscotland.org.uk/__data/assets/pdf_file/0011/650/westminster_confession.pdf. Accessed 15 October 2010.
4. See note 2 above. The preface to the Scots Confession of 1560 made the same point.

5 http://www.churchofscotland.org.uk/about_us/our_faith/statements_of_the_churchs_faith. Accessed 15 October 2010. The Apostles' Creed had been an integral part of 'Knox's Liturgy' or 'Forme of Prayers', later designated as the *Book of Common Order*. The original Panel on Doctrine Report and Assembly Statement are much more nuanced

6 Finlay Macdonald, 'Understanding our present – anticipating the future', *Theology in Scotland* 17:2 (2010), p. 102.

7 C[harles] G. McCrie, *The Confessions of the Church of Scotland: Their Evolution and History. The Seventh Series of the Chalmers Lectures* (Edinburgh: MacNiven & Wallace, 1907), p. 258 and note 1 there. In 1788, the American Presbyterian Church had revised the chapters in respect of relations with the civil authority. By McCrie's own time, some United Free churchmen – above all, the influential Glasgow United Free Church College Principal, James Denney – were radically minimalist on the matter of a confession of faith.

8 'Calvin in Scotland', *Theology in Scotland* 17:2 (2010), p. 80.

9 G. D. Henderson, *Scots Confession 1560 (Confessio Scoticana) and Negative Confession, 1581 (Confessio Negativa)* (Edinburgh: Church of Scotland Publications Committee, 1937).

10 See Bibliography below, under Hazlett, item 1.

11 McCrie, *The Confessions*, p. 35.

12 'A declaracion or wytnessynge of our mynde.' See *Miscellany of the Wodrow Society*, ed. David Laing (Edinburgh: Wodrow Society, 1844), p. 23.

13 *Scots Confession 1560 … and Negative Confession, 1581…*, p. 35.

14 Adam Milroy, quoted by Donald Macmillan, *The Aberdeen Doctors: A Notable Group of Scottish Theologians of the First Episcopal Period, 1610–1638* (London: Hodder & Stoughton, 1909), p. 98.

15 Cf. W. R. Foster, *The Church before the Covenants: The Church of Scotland 1596–1638* (Edinburgh and London: Scottish Academic Press, 1975), pp. 12–31; W. Brown Patterson, *King James VI and I and the Reunion of Christendom* (Cambridge: Cambridge University Press, 1997), pp. 8–12.

16 First published out of the General Assembly's original register or records (no longer extant) in David Calderwood's posthumous *The True History of the Church of Scotland …* (1678), pp. 668–73. This short history of the Kirk (by Calderwood's standards) was reprinted in 1680 and 1704. The confession was published later in *The Book of the Universall Kirk of Scotland / Acts and Proceedings of the General Assemblies of the Kirk of Scotland, Part Third*, ed. Thomas Thomson (Edinburgh: The Maitland Club, 1845), pp. 132–9. See now a modernised version in Duncan Shaw (ed.), *The Acts and Proceedings of the General Assemblies of the Church of Scotland 1560 to 1618*, Publications of the Scottish Record Society, new series, 26–8 (Edinburgh: Scottish Record Society, 2004), vol. 3, pp. 523–31.

17 Cf. William Scot, *An Apologetical Narration of the State and Government of the Church of Scotland since the Reformation* (Edinburgh: The Wodrow Society, 1846), p. 243.

Bibliography

Barth, Karl, *The Knowledge of God and the Service of God according to the Teaching of the Reformation* [Aberdeen Gifford Lectures on the Scots Confession], trans. James L. M. Haire and Ian Henderson (London: Hodder & Stoughton, 1938).

Calderwood, David, *The True History of the Church of Scotland* (1678).

Calderwood, David, *The History of the Kirk of Scotland*, ed. Thomas Thomson, 8 vols (Edinburgh: The Wodrow Society, 1845).

Cheyne, Alec, 'The Scots Confession of 1560', *Theology Today* 17 (1960), pp. 323–38.

Chisholm, William, *Examen confessionis fidei Caluiniae, quam Scotis omnibus Ministri Caluiniani subscribendam et iurandum proponunt* (Avignon, 1601). [French trans. by Nicolas Coeffeteau: *Examen d'une confession de foy* (Paris, 1603).]

Cochrane, Arthur C. (ed.), *Reformed Confessions of the 16th Century, with historical introductions* (London: SCM Press, 1966). [Reissued with new intro. by Jack Rogers (Louisville, KY: Westminster John Knox Press, 2003).]

Cooper, James, *Confessions of Faith and Formulas of Subscription in the Reformed Churches of Great Britain and Ireland especially in the Church of Scotland* (Glasgow: James Maclehose & Sons, 1907).

Cowan, Ian, 'The Five Articles of Perth', in Duncan Shaw (ed.), *Reformation and Revolution: Essays Presented to the Very Reverend Hugh Watt* (Edinburgh: Saint Andrew Press, 1967), pp. 160–7.

Fergusson, David, 'Calvin in Scotland', *Theology in Scotland* 17:2 (2010), pp. 67–81.

Ford, John D., 'The lawful bonds of Scottish society: the Five Articles of Perth, the Negative Confession and the National Covenant', *The Historical Journal* 37:1 (1994), pp. 45–64.

Foster, Walter Roland, *The Church before the Covenants: The Church of Scotland 1596–1638* (Edinburgh and London: Scottish Academic Press, 1975).

Gribben, Crawford, 'Scottish theological literature, 1560–1707', in Ian Brown et al. (eds), *The Edinburgh History of Scottish Literature:*

From Columba to the Union (until 1707) (Edinburgh: Edinburgh University Press, 2006), pp. 213–37.

Hazlett, Ian (ed.), 'Confessio Scotica 1560', in Andreas Mühling and Peter Opitz (gen. eds), *Reformierte Bekenntnisschriften*, vol. 2/1, *1559–1563* (Neukirchen-Vluyn: Neukirchener, 2009), pp. 209–300.

Hazlett, Ian, 'A new version of the Scots Confession, 1560', *Theology in Scotland* 17:2 (2010), pp. 33–66.

Hazlett, Ian (ed.), 'Confessio Scotica posterior, 1581', in Andreas Mühling and Peter Opitz (gen. eds), *Reformierte Bekenntnisschriften*, vol. 3/1, *1570–1595* (Neukirchen-Vluyn: Neukirchener, 2012), pp. 185–228.

Henderson, G. D., *Scots Confession 1560 (Confessio Scoticana) and Negative Confession, 1581 (Confessio Negativa)* (Edinburgh: Church of Scotland Publications Committee, 1937).

Innes, Alexander Taylor, *The Law of Creeds in Scotland* (Edinburgh and London, 1868).

McCrie, Charles G., *The Confessions of the Church of Scotland: Their Evolution and History. The Seventh Series of the Chalmers Lectures* (Edinburgh: MacNiven & Wallace, 1907).

Macdonald, Alan R., 'James VI and I, the Church of Scotland, and British ecclesiastical convergence', *The Historical Journal* 48:4 (2005), pp. 885–903.

Macdonald, Finlay, 'Understanding our present – anticipating the future', *Theology in Scotland* 17:2 (2010), pp. 83–93.

MacMillan, Donald, *The Aberdeen Doctors: A Notable Group of Scottish Theologians of the First Episcopal Period, 1610–1638* (London: Hodder & Stoughton, 1909).

Patterson, W. Brown, *King James VI and I and the Reunion of Christendom* (Cambridge: Cambridge University Press, 1997).

Pelikan, Jaroslav and Valerie Hotchkiss (eds), *Creeds and Confessions of Faith in the Christian Tradition*, vol. 2, pt 4: *Creeds and Confessions in the Reformation Era* (New Haven and London: Yale University Press, 2003).

Rohls, Jan, *Reformed Confessions: Theology from Zurich to Barmen* (Louisville, KY: Westminster John Knox Press, 1998).

Scot, William, *An Apologetical Narration of the State and Government of the Church of Scotland since the Reformation* (Edinburgh: The Wodrow Society, 1846).

Shaw, Duncan (ed.), *The Acts and Proceedings of the General Assemblies of the Church of Scotland 1560 to 1618*, 3 vols. Publications of the Scottish Record Society, new series, pp. 26–8 (Edinburgh: Scottish Record Society, 2004).

Spottiswoode, John, *History of the Church of Scotland … in Seven Books* [1655], [*Book VI, anno 1580*], ed. M. Napier and M. Russell, 3 vols (Edinburgh: Spottiswoode Society, 1847–51).

Stevenson, David, *King's College, Aberdeen, 1560–1641: From Protestant Reformation to Covenanting Revolution* (Aberdeen: Aberdeen University Press, 1990).

Thomson, Thomas (ed.), *The Book of the Universall Kirk of Scotland / Acts and Proceedings of the General Assemblies of the Kirk of Scotland, Part Third* (Edinburgh: The Maitland Club, 1845).

Torrance, Thomas, 'The substance of faith', in David Willis-Watkins and Michael Welker (eds), *Toward the Future of Reformed Theology: Tasks, Topics, Traditions* (Grand Rapids: Eerdmans, 1999), pp. 167–77. [Originally entitled 'The substance of the faith', in *Scottish Journal of Theology* 36 (1983), pp. 327–38.]

Wormald, Jenny, '"No bishop, no king": the Scottish Jacobean episcopate, 1600–1635', in Bernard Vogler (ed.), *Bibliothèque de la Revue d'Histoire Ecclésiastique*, 68: *Miscellanea Historiae Ecclesiasticae*, VIII (Brussels: Nauwelaerts, 1987), pp. 259–67.

Wright, David F., 'The Scottish Reformation: theology and theologians', in David Bagchi and David C. Steinmetz (eds), *The Cambridge Companion to Reformation Theology* (Cambridge: Cambridge University Press, 2004), pp. 174–93.

UNCOMMON ORDER?

Possible futures of worship in the Church of Scotland[1]

DOUG GAY

With a title which promises futures, readers should be forewarned that what follows contains a good deal of reflection on the past. I am increasingly convinced of the importance for contemporary practical theological reflection on worship and liturgy of the story we tell ourselves about our past. Some recent writers speak of the importance of what they call a 'useable past' – a term which acknowledges the way in which we construct and deploy readings of history in the service of our own practice.

Those taking on the Chalmers lectureship are engaged to explore their theme in relation to the Kingship of Christ over the Church – and in my case, there was no awkwardness about complying with that, since there is an intimate connection between the church's worship and the reign of Christ the King.

In fact, I want to begin there, by reflecting on the importance of understanding the rule and reign of Jesus Christ within his church, as a gracious and generous rule and reign. The lecture of which this paper is a version was delivered on the great festival day of Pentecost. At Pentecost, we celebrate both the ascension of Jesus Christ and his recognition as high king of heaven, and we celebrate also what comes with it, the coming of the Holy Spirit and the giving of gifts to the church. As the hymn says: the

The ascended Christ with the Holy Spirit (the Dove) issuing from him and descending on the gathered community is focal for the congregation of Paisley Abbey in the Great East Window.

Detail from the central portion of the Great East Window. Photo: J. Law

High King of Heaven is the one who is our inheritance and our treasure.

If we look to Ephesians 4, it is the ascended Christ who gives gifts to his people, above all the giving gift of the co-equal, co-eternal one who proceeds from the Father and the Son – the same Holy Spirit whose coming we celebrate at Pentecost. The Kingship of Christ can be distinguished from, but may not be separated from, the Lordship of the Spirit.

I begin with this remembering of the *charismata*, of the 'gifts of grace' given by Christ through the Holy Spirit, because some of what I want to go on and say is deliberately quite specific. It is intended to be critical in the reflective, academic sense of that word, but I am aware that some of it may also be seen as critical in a narrower and sharper sense. It is because of this that I want to emphasise at the beginning the importance of a theology of worship in which we rely completely on the grace of God.

The danger of any attempt to improve, refine or develop worship practice within the church is that it falls over into a prideful or pelagian understanding of worship in which we are somehow trying to impress one another or even impress God with our offerings. That is a real danger and one which can surface from many different angles within the life of the Kirk – it needs to be met with a real humility and a theological and spiritual understanding of worship in which the grace of our Lord Jesus Christ is decisive.

We depend on the grace of God – and on the promise 'draw near to God and God will draw near to you' (James 4:8). This means we need to be always aware that, in the many thousands of acts of public worship in the Church of Scotland each week, there will be examples which we might consider to be boring, scrappy, unimaginative and narrow or alternatively showy, self-indulgent, pompous and superficial. Very often, in a system like ours, those judgements will be judgements largely on ministerial practice – but praise God, God does 'show up', God graciously draws near to congregations and to individual worshippers even in conditions where we, if we were the Holy Spirit, might take a scunner and hold ourselves back. That should be a warning to us, where we might disdain or discount what is taking place in worship.

There is a corollary, where we might feel a flush of pride about how sound, or creative or beautiful, how anointed or cutting-edge or politically engaged our practice might be. It may still be that God's response to our worship will be as in Amos 5:23 'away with your noisy songs'; it may be that God's response to our worship will be as in Matthew 7:23 'I never knew you'; or it may be that God's response to our worship will be as in 1 Corinthians 11:17 'in this matter you do more harm than good', or as in Revelation 2 'I will remove your lampstand from its place', or Revelation 3 'I will spit you out of my mouth'. That too should be a warning to us, where we might trust in our works and presume upon the approval of God.

With those caveats hanging over us, let me move on and risk bringing them down on my own head by offering some critical thoughts on worship practice.

2010 combined two anniversaries – the 450th of the Reformation settlement and the 100th of the Edinburgh 1910 World Missionary Conference – hailed as the birth of the modern ecumenical movement. It provided us with an opportunity to reflect on three themes which are crucially important to the future of the Church of Scotland and not least to its worship – reformed identity, mission, and ecumenical commitment.

From 1562 onwards, the Church of Scotland has used the term 'Common Order' as a way of expressing its concern that there should be at least a family resemblance between acts of public worship within the Kirk, both in what was included and excluded, without wholly fixing or restricting the content of reformed liturgy according to a detailed liturgical canon or prayer book.

There have to date been four major editions of a *Book of Common Order* – those produced variously in 1562, 1940, 1979 and 1994. The time-slip of almost four centuries between the first and second books tells its own story about the evolution of worship practice within the Kirk. This was pithily summarised by Howard Hageman when, speaking of written liturgies, he claimed that 'Reformed liturgies proliferated in the 16th century, died in the 17th century and were buried in the 18th'.[2]

Within the Church of Scotland, we might speak of three liturgical eras leading up to the 400th anniversary of the Scottish Reformation Settlement in 1960. The first, from 1560 to the 1630s, we might describe as an era of *reformation*; the second, from the 1640s to the 1830s, we might describe as an era of *reduction* – both in the sense of loss of variety and, in the Delia Smith sense, of concentration and intensification. The third era, dating from the middle decades of the Victorian era to the mid-twentieth century, we might describe as an era of *recovery* and of *revival* in which the worship practices of the Kirk began increasingly to reflect the work of the 'Scoto-Catholic' liturgical campaigners on the one hand and, on the other, the new repertoires and techniques of the evangelical, Methodist/Congregationalist and Pentecostalist insurgencies.

All three of these eras, as well as the more hybrid, varied and diverse era which the Kirk has lived through from 1960 to 2010, have left their mark on its worship, and all have an ongoing legacy which affects how we think about the future.

The sixteenth-century *reformation* of worship marked Reformed worship decisively, for good and for ill. The radical turn to the vernacular, the rise of congregational singing and the massive promotion of preaching combined with a new communal enactment of the Lord's Supper, where, as Margo Todd points out, the Laird left his pew and literally moved to sit beside the

Preacher and precentor in the double pulpit in Tolbooth Church, Edinburgh.

labourer at the table in a way perhaps unmatched at any other dinner table in Scotland.[3] A book of common order, purged of many Roman elements and with a radically simplified liturgy, nevertheless held on to a basic liturgical structure which showed some continuity with the Western rite and which made room for 'free' prayer without abolishing certain key set elements. On the negative side, the sixteenth-century changes enshrined a deep suspicion of ritual and of the visual arts and maintained a clerical and male monopoly over most of the leadership of worship. They also failed in their declared aim of establishing frequent communion and, arguably, produced an unconvincing theology of infant baptism.

The seventeenth- and eighteenth-century era of *reduction* in worship saw these trends concentrated further – the bitterness of early seventeenth-century struggles over the imposition of bishops, rubrics and prayer books prepared the ground for taking on the Westminster Directory as an indicative standard for worship. The Westminster pattern reinforced a puritan austerity and reserve in Presbyterian worship, leaving the sermon and extempore prayers as the main liturgical outlet for the creative energies and instincts of ministers. The ambitions for more frequent celebration of the Lord's Supper were largely set aside; and the way in which the regulatory principle was applied to congregational song meant that Scottish Presbyterians, restricted to the Psalms, could not join fully in the eighteenth-century explosion of Protestant hymnody, at least in their main worship services. The eighteenth-century division of the Kirk into moderate and evangelical camps did not really challenge the austerity of the liturgical patterns; it simply offered a choice between more refined and more impassioned styles of rhetoric. The exception to this might be if we were to read some of the famous eighteenth-century revivals as anticipations of Pentecostalism, which, like the early Methodism they were contemporary with, began to break open a clergy-centred worship tradition by allowing room for spirit-filled contributions from a wider group of lay people.

The era of reduction, in its attempts to intensify the spirit of Calvin and Knox, ironically moved away from their practices in some key respects. Both Evangelicals and Moderates in their different ways journeyed further into a resolutely plain style in everything apart from verbal rhetoric – and a basic pattern of worship in which the balance between word and sacrament was scarcely kept in respect of communion, with frequency in individual parishes falling below annual levels in some places.

When we move into our third era, the period of liturgical retrieval and revival beginning in the nineteenth century, we find the beginning of two distinct streams, which flow on into the twentieth century and which continue to shape the main options in contemporary worship practice within the Church of Scotland today.

The first of those streams is best described as 'Evangelical', so long as we realise that term undergoes significant changes in meaning between the eighteenth and twentieth centuries.[4] It takes the initial impulses of the early Reformers, received through the more austere filters of Puritanism, and sees them gradually warmed or perhaps even strangely warmed through the influence of pietism and romanticism. The worship culture which develops is unmistakably low-church in its suspicion of ritual and prayer books, but it finds a new expressive capacity in first the congregational hymn and then the evangelical chorus. While the art of the hymn had developed its own refinements in the hands of a Watt or a Wesley, in evangelical circles there was always to be a lean towards the popular. Moody and Sankey brought the music hall to the tent hall, Golden Bells chimed sweetly, and CSSM and Scripture Union choruses were sung first at seaside missions and later in church evening services. Having denied itself the solemn ritual, pomp and ceremony of the higher classic/catholic traditions, the aesthetic deficit

The organ, now in Canongate Kirk, that Sankey played on one of his Edinburgh missions.

Photo: Neil Gardner

which had built up in the seventeenth and eighteenth centuries was made up for from the nineteenth century in a greater capacity to appropriate and engage with the forms of popular culture. The approval of both hymn-singing and instrumental accompaniment for this found enthusiastic support within this broader project.

Inevitably, that cultural trajectory carries associations of class and taste with it: it is seen as more hearty and populist, more petit bourgeois and working-class. There have doubtless been many anticipations over the past 200 years of Richard Holloway's more recent and fabulously snobbish *bon mot*: 'Why do evangelicals have to have such bad taste?'[5]

Within the Church of Scotland, even throughout most of the twentieth century, more conservative figures in this reinvented evangelical tradition held to a Sunday pattern which in cultural and liturgical terms remained cautious and austere, though not without its own warmth and passion. The intensely worked and delivered expository sermon remained central to worship. Even into the 1980s, in a Gilcomston South, a Holyrood Abbey or a St George's Tron, the more populist elements would be restricted to the youth or children's settings, to camps or conventions. A more modernising strain of evangelicals had long been committed to making maximum use of such elements to enhance the cultural appeal of gospel presentations. From the 1930s onwards, beginning with evening services, but spreading to morning worship via the children's talk and hymn, the popular evangelical repertoire began to add its appeal and vigour to Presbyterian Sundays. While its critics might wonder how Reformed its liturgical instincts were, the strength of an accompanying preaching tradition was usually enough to keep them at bay.

The second great stream, spreading out from the nineteenth-century Kirk, although rather less so from the Free Kirk, was the movement to revive and recover a 'higher' form of Presbyterian worship, which understood itself to be simultaneously catholic and reformed. Under the influence of a wider cultural fashion that we call 'romanticism', Presbyterians tired of the era of reduction and of liturgical austerity, and began to refurbish their liturgical practice with elements from the earliest patterns of Reformed worship, alongside borrowings from Episcopalian and Catholic practice. Long-standing taboos about musical accompaniment were overcome, as a way of linking into a broad classical tradition of church music and hymnody was increasingly welcomed. Other taboos also began to fall: church festivals, high days and holy weeks, ritual, kneeling for prayer, set forms of prayer with congregational responses, candles and vestments – only a few places embraced all these changes, but the rise of the Church Service Society from the 1860s bore witness to a growing appetite for a more catholic form of Presbyterianism.

The production of the 1940 *Book of Common Order*, to considerable international and ecumenical acclaim, was the high point of Scoto-Catholic achievement within the Church of Scotland. A decade after the Glorious Union of 1929, it announced a new sensibility to the world, which was dignified, catholic and reformed. It too carried associations of class and taste – offering at last what was seen as a more refined and culturally enlightened diet for Presbyterian worship. It allowed the Church to occupy a more confident space within a newly burgeoning ecumenical movement and conversation. Already, however, there were question marks about how common this new order was. Many evangelicals simply ignored the 1940 book, as they would have done any book, but especially one as Scoto-Catholic as this one. They had every right to do so, and they exercised that right freely.

The last fifty years, from 1960 to 2010, have seen a more hybrid, varied and diverse set of patterns emerge within the worship of the Church of Scotland.

To understand this period and how it is likely to influence the future, it is necessary to note two other distinct but related variations of evangelicalism – the rise of Pentecostalism from the early twentieth century and the spread of the Charismatic Renewal from the 1960s onwards. In terms of liturgy, the influence of both these movements has been in a 'low'-church direction, with their emphasis on the work of the Holy Spirit reanimating sixteenth- and seventeenth-century oppositions between set liturgy and free or extempore prayer. They have also continued the cultural pattern within evangelicalism of embracing forms of popular culture, particularly musical forms. In the case of Pentecostalism, it was influenced from the beginning by African-American musical

'Rhythm and physical movement'. The choir from Scottish African churches at the closing session of 'Edinburgh 2010', a conference to mark the centenary of the World Missionary Conference in Edinburgh in 1910.

© Gary Doak

traditions which emphasised rhythm, physical movement and expressive use of the body. In the case of the Charismatic Renewal, it inherited both the example of Pentecostal worship styles, but also the influence of gospel music as a developed liturgical form and the rise of rock 'n' roll to become an international mass art form and expressive culture. As with previous engagements with popular culture, both of these movements have often been harshly judged by other sections of the Church in terms of the aesthetic and spiritual value of their choices. Overall, the direct influence of Pentecostalism and Charismatic Renewal on the liturgical patterns and theology of individual Church of Scotland congregations has been relatively low compared to, say, its influence on the Church of England, but its indirect influence on attitudes to worship and on the repertoire of congregational song has been very far-reaching and continues to grow. That said, within the Church of Scotland, there have continued to be a good number of conservative evangelical congregations which have actively resisted the influence of the charismatic renewal, both theologically and liturgically. (But even St George's Tron now has an electric bass guitar at morning worship.)

The story of our other catholic/ecumenical stream also has its own set of variations on that theme. Although many people are gloomy about the current state of ecumenism, the story of worship across mainstream, 'oldline' Church traditions in the last 150 years is a remarkable story of ecumenical convergence. This convergence has been fed by the Liturgical Movement, a broadly based, often highly academic conversation about the history and practice of worship, which has had a huge influence over the revision of approved liturgical texts, missals, books of common prayer and books of common order. The US Episcopal scholar Patrick Malloy puts it like this:

> After more than one hundred years of research, fermentation and experimentation the late twentieth century saw the creation of new liturgies that drew heavily on the historical, liturgical and theological evidence that the Liturgical Movement had unearthed and explored.

Setting aside the question of whether the liturgical tradition of the early Church deserves such emulation, it is clear that these new liturgies bear a striking resemblance; some are essentially indistinguishable, despite crossing denominational lines. Along with the similarity in the rites themselves, a common ecumenical liturgical vision has emerged. The polemics of the Reformation are not resolved, but they have generally receded behind a shared theology and a shared understanding of how liturgy is to be enacted and why. More than at any time since the Reformation, in the twenty-first century it is now possible to discern a Western normative liturgical pattern.

Malloy also goes on to speak about 'the ecumenical consensus that has steadily emerged during the past fifty years'.[6]

Within the Church of Scotland, the Church Service Society remains a crucial channel for the influence of this consensus, and the 1994 *Book of Common Order* both reflects it and is highly self-conscious about how far it does so.

Alongside this public and formal process of producing official, authorised revisions of liturgical texts, there have been three other key variations which must be mentioned.

The first is the influence of the Taizé Community – a striking example of a Protestant foundation which fell in love with Catholic tradition and which produced a remarkable set of worked examples of how to adapt the work of the Liturgical Movement for a new generation. Taizé worked in a less tightly

'We are marching in the light of God'.

regulated space alongside the main European churches, where it was more able to experiment – its reworking of liturgical chant as a participative and popular art form was hugely influential between the 1970s and the 1990s.

In parallel with Taizé, we find the work of Scotland's and the Church of Scotland's own Iona Community. Impelled by the same love of Catholic tradition, allowed a similar space alongside the Church to experiment and take risks, and inspired by the work of two outstanding liturgical poets and thinkers, George MacLeod and John Bell – Iona has become an international liturgical phenomenon. Almost single-handedly, the Wild Goose project in recent years has transformed Scotland's liturgical balance of payments, exporting material – both liturgies and songs – all over the world.

Finally, and not unrelated to these other two, has been the influence of the World Council of Churches and the liturgical sharing between cultures and hemispheres enabled and inspired through its gatherings and assemblies. The rise of a more political ecumenism from the 1960s onwards raised awareness of the politics of worship. It not only reflected on the cultural imperialism of the worship practices introduced by Western missions, it also inspired a 'reverse mission', post-colonial exchange of practices and resources. Just as Alexander Duff might have taught *Jesus shall reign where'er the sun* to nineteenth-century Indian converts in Calcutta, so late twentieth-century Presbyterians in Auchterarder or Kilmacolm learned to sing *Siyahamba – We are marching in the light of God*.

We noted above that criticisms of evangelical practice carried assumptions about class and culture – and likewise, criticisms of this Catholic/ecumenical stream have suggested that the Scoto-Catholic agenda was both elitist and pretentious and not without a certain liturgical 'campness'. Taizé's fondness for Latin and Greek was seen as a Euro-Catholic affectation, and its infatuation with slow classical music was seen as ponderous and out of touch with contemporary culture. Iona's folkiness was seen to smack of beard-wearing, real-ale-drinking eccentricity; and its more recent love affair with world music was derided for allowing liberals (who hated evangelical choruses) to sing simplistic love songs to Jesus, so long as they were in an African indigenous language which they didn't understand …

The end result of this brief attempt to construct a story about worship in the Church of Scotland is, for me, a serious question about the meaning of common order. What is it? And does it exist?

Is Common Order a normative pattern for worship in the Church of Scotland – and, if so, who says it is normative? Would it be just as legitimate and more fruitful to simply ask: which order is most common, which forms are most commonly used?

As we look at the present and look to the future, say to the next ten or twenty years of worship practice in the Church of Scotland, I suggest we will go on wrestling with the divided liturgical mind of the Kirk. In particular, we will continue to see these two dynamics at work – of ecumenical convergence and evangelical distinctiveness. And we will continue to see enthusiasts on both sides look at one another sometimes with distaste and other times with real incomprehension.

The US scholar Frank Burch Brown has directed our attention in recent years to the issue of 'taste', which is helpful because questions of taste are often not well discussed within the Church or made the subject of serious theological reflection.[7] But there are signs that, in relation to these two dynamics, very different tastes are hardening on both sides in ways that give cause for concern – for example, one side cares little for whether there has been a formal *epiklesis* in the communion prayer; the other believes the use of screens for PowerPoint projection to be an abomination …

Those who understand common order as a coherent catholic and reformed liturgical pattern, revised and refined in conversation with ecumenical partners, have, as Patrick Malloy suggests, achieved a great deal in the twentieth century – it is understandable that they should point to the developing ecumenical consensus post-Vatican II and find 'Common Order' being both rediscovered and deepened in exciting ways.

Those who are left cold by this are likely to point out that, on the ground, churchgoers are voting with their feet – and the fastest-growing churches, predicted to make up an ever larger percentage of all Scotland's congregations and all Church of Scotland congregations in the next twenty years, are the progressive or charismatic evangelical churches. Their new version of common order involves informally introduced worship, building through an extended period of 'praise and worship' – highly expressive and emotionally charged congregational songs, interwoven with short extempore prayers – all of this commonly led by someone other than the ordained minister – opening into a sermon space, which may be anything from twenty to forty minutes – and which may be followed by a time of response, featuring more extempore prayer, more singing and opportunities for people to come forward and receive individual 'ministry' as people pray for them and lay hands on them.

In fact, both of these trends in worship practice within the Kirk can be seen to be driven by similar concerns – a desire to go beyond the dull and plain formula of minister-centred worship on the Westminster Directory model. Increasingly, the Church of Scotland is tired of the age of liturgical austerity – there is a hunger for more variety, colour and experiential engagement. Both our streams offer this, but do so in very different ways. And both are vulnerable to criticism – the 'catholic' strand is vulnerable to accusations of elitism and irrelevance; the charismatic evangelical strand to accusations of banality and superficiality.

In this final section, I want to offer ten theses about possible futures of worship in the Church of Scotland.

1. *The age of (liturgical) austerity is over*

The bog-standard minister-dominated hymn sandwich, devoid of all set liturgy other than the Lord's Prayer, and with the people's part reduced to this and singing hymns, is on its way out. We should both celebrate this and speed its demise. There is one exception. In some churches which have particularly strong and intense preaching traditions – I think particularly of conservative evangelical churches – the emotional and spiritual drama of the sermon plus extempore prayers is still powerful enough for worshippers to feel that it carries the rest of the service. Where it is not, the persistence of this standard-issue, middle-of-the-road Presbyterian service is dragging the Kirk down deeper into decline and cultural irrelevance.

2. *Ecumenical convergence is here to stay, but its champions have choices to make*

The long process of ecumenical convergence has grown in influence and in confidence. Its capture of official service books and its dominance in liturgical scholarship and teaching ensures that its voice will continue to be strong. However, it is weakened by its tendency to prioritise worship over mission, by its failure when implemented within many local congregations to enable congregational growth – and sometimes by its own timidity. If a Scoto-Catholic Presbyterian is simply a poor man's Episcopalian, why not skip the Kirk and opt for the real thing?

Two future options suggest themselves. One is for more local unions with Scottish Episcopal congregations which recognise their common ground and work on a new hybrid model. The second is for advocates of ecumenical convergence to get over their own preciousness and work with emerging church networks, many of whom have a strong interest in recovering classic, catholic practices within a new congregational mix. A question here is whether we could cope with a future where a strong vision of 'common order' was linked to a more flexible vision of ordination and presidency. The paradoxical danger facing high-church Presbyterians is that, while their case is strengthening, their support base is shrinking. I suspect membership figures for the Church Service Society might confirm that.

There are also strong signs among the poorest sections of Scottish society that charismatic-evangelical worship is one of the very few options which can still engage and attract people and accompany church growth. There is therefore an increasing danger that, in the near future, 'high-church Presbyterianism', even in its Iona form, will become mainly an option for the chattering classes.

3. *Evangelicalism is set to grow, but its proponents have lessons to learn*

If we believe both existing trends and those who make predictions, the future is evangelical, with evangelical congregations within the Church of Scotland outgrowing, outplanting and outlasting others, while also generating more candidates for ministry. This will happen against an overall picture of continuing decline, meaning that evangelicals will form an ever greater percentage of the total.

Success plus growth can immunise us against reform. The challenge here is for evangelicals to be more reflective about worship and more ready to reform their own liturgical practice, rather than to simply stick with a winning formula. It is a challenge to re-examine the opposition between set forms and spiritual freedom – not least by looking back to the earliest Reformation patterns.[8] It is a challenge to conservatives to be more creative: between 1940 and 2010, how many new hymns and praise songs were written by people within the Crieff circle of churches, and how many were welcomed in from outside?

There are signs here of a decadent form of conservatism, which relies on the creativity of previous generations but refuses to nurture or risk its own.[9]

For charismatic evangelicals, there are different challenges. One is well presented by Pete Ward in his book *Selling Worship*, which is to work for greater quality and wider theological range in their worship songs.[10] Again, our theological colleges and candidate/probationer conferences are very weak in both scholarship and teaching in this area. We need to invest time, money and energy in changing this. One final question is the rise of options, some associated with an emerging-church agenda, called things like 'café church', 'messy church', 'fresh church' … which have, in common, a huge premium being placed upon informality. Informality is not the highest value in worship, and sometimes it is the enemy of fitting worship. There is a need to challenge cultural suspicions of ritual, form and order within charismatic evangelical churches.

4. *The future involves more frequent communion*

I predicted this in my concluding chapter to the 2009 book I edited with Duncan Forrester[11] – and it is fair to say that eyebrows have been raised. The reason I think it *will* come is because it is one of a few areas of common ground between our two streams; both Scoto-Catholics and Evangelicals tend to favour frequent celebration of the Lord's Supper. The reason I think it *should* come is that, while it is no magic formula, I believe that at this point in time it can be an antidote to both the plainness and the wordiness of Presbyterian worship. Our increasingly divided and atomised society needs tables where we can sit together and circles where we can stand together. How we celebrate seems likely to change as well. In my experience, younger generations of worshippers are drawn to the common cup and loaf. We will

Heart & Soul, a 'celebration of the life of the Church', which takes place in Princes Street Gardens on the Sunday of the General Assembly each year, is gathered up in an act of worship on the main stage.

© *James Hogg*

be wise to open up our practice to allow flows of change, even if individual cups and common cups have to co-exist for a while within congregations.

5. *The future of baptism in a post-Christendom Scotland looks different from its past*

If communion has a powerful cultural resonance and even a missional appeal, baptism is emerging as a more problematic cultural ritual; and its connections to 'confirmation' and receiving communion are becoming less clear to many within the Kirk. I say to my students: either you will baptise more adults than any other generation of Church of Scotland ministers, or the Church as we know it is finished. The transition from the early norm of baptism of adults by immersion to universal baptism of infants by pouring led to major liturgical and architectural changes. In the same way, the growing post-Christendom trend of increased numbers of adult baptisms will call for changes in liturgy and practice, and in buildings too, and for the revival of catechesis – perhaps through Alpha-style groups? The service of thanksgiving and blessing for infants has already become an established pastoral and liturgical option within the Kirk. Is it possible that this will mark an interim stage on a journey towards a URC-like position on baptism, possibly as part of a future organic union with the National Synod of Scotland? Certainly, in the face of a continuing massive and rapid decline in the number of infants being brought for baptism in Scotland – if the Church grows again, or where it grows again, baptism of adults on profession of faith will acquire an unprecedented significance in the life of the Kirk.

6. *Preaching is not going away, so we need to get better at it*

In respect of preaching, the Church of Scotland is living off a reputation, which is still strong in other parts of the world but which it no longer deserves at home. We have too many ministers in post who can't preach well, who were given little support in this area during training, and who are not clear how to improve their practice. When your most common Sunday order invests so much in the sermon, this is potentially disastrous. We need a ten-year programme of investment in homiletical training within the Church of Scotland, and we need ministers humble enough to participate in it. We need to build capacity in homiletics in at least one of our Church colleges and to develop ways of extending this to a broader programme of continuing ministerial education.

7. *Worship culture is becoming more visual, so we need to reflect, train for and resource this*

We have already moved from a predominantly print culture to a new oral/visual era. This is reflected both in the renewed emphasis upon symbol and ritual in catholic/reformed/ emerging circles and in the rise of video projection screens in evangelical churches. These changes should be understood in relation to a developing theological concern for the importance of 'embodied worship'.[12] Future education and training in liturgy and worship will need to reflect these changes and give critical attention to them and to the opportunities and pitfalls they bring.

8. *The future involves a new and enhanced role for lay people in leading worship*

From the missionary movements of the nineteenth century to the pioneering work of J. H. Oldham in the 1930s and of Hendrik Kraemer in the 1950s, the role of 'the laity' continues to trouble the waters in relation to liturgy and worship. Today we have the ecumenical irony of Roman Catholic order allowing for lay people to be Eucharistic ministers, while Presbyterian order risks reinforcing the famine of communion in the Kirk. The Church of England has trained and ordained thousands of non-stipendiary ministers in recent decades to maintain Eucharistic ministries, but NSMs remain a tiny minority in the Church of Scotland. We may hope that the introduction of Ordained Local Ministry from 2011 will address this, but we must also be wary of it further reinforcing a clericalism which will limit the missional imagination and capacity of Presbyterian congregations. It is vital that this is complemented by a new openness to the contribution of lay people in worship and a new commitment to training and resourcing them.

The visual dimension. Palm trees made from colourful fabric sent ahead by delegates from many countries surrounded participants throughout the Edinburgh 2010 conference. Individual leaves were embroidered with messages of peace and with the titles of the songs of the conference in many languages. They were designed and constructed by Carol Marples of the Scottish-based Soul Marks Trust.

9. *Those leading worship in future will have to expect and respond to much lower levels of biblical literacy*

Levels of biblical literacy are declining exponentially within contemporary culture, while the use of an increasing number of translations continues to erode a common memory of the text. This change brings with it great challenges for preachers and liturgists. One significant response is the E-100 project from the UK and US Bible Societies. But desktop publishing and new electronic media are also offering new opportunities to present the text on screen and in orders of service to worshippers and seekers who may not be bible-carriers.

10. *Many congregations will have fewer children and young people in church*

One of the consequences of severe decline in rates of baptism, membership and attendance across Scotland is that the number of children and young people has reached unprecedentedly low levels in many congregations. This brings great anguish for many within our churches, and in terms of prospects for growth it is near-disastrous, especially when the Sunday School ceases and this becomes a deterrent to new families joining. There are signs of a new attentiveness to the issues involved in 'children's ministry' and some important ecumenical flows between denominations in sharing new patterns of 'children's liturgy'. Some tensions exist between passionate exponents of 'inclusion' and passionate opponents of 'dumbing down'. In the Kirk, the spread of children at communion and the decline of teenagers 'joining the Church' is creating theological and pastoral confusion about patterns and sequences of Christian initiation. In the next two decades, the presence (and absence) of children in the Church's worship will need continuing and thoughtful attention.

Conclusion

In 2011, we have to face the possibility that Common Order no longer really exists in the Church of Scotland. If this is so, it will have to be rebuilt – and, while I believe it *could* be rebuilt better than before, I am not confident it *will* be. I have not said much about 'emerging church' concerns, as I have addressed this in my book *Remixing the Church*. There, I reflect on how churches change through auditing, retrieval, unbundling, supplementing and finally remixing – creating new combinations of identity and practice, not least in the area of worship. My enthusiasm for the emerging agenda reflects my belief in the ongoing need for cross-fertilisation as we seek to discern how to shape future patterns of worship in the Kirk. Like the Edinburgh Festival, official ecumenism has always been surrounded by a much larger informal 'fringe' made up of thousands of sites where creative experiments are taking place and old classics are being revived. Perhaps that is not such a bad metaphor for Common Order in the Kirk. We can find it both in the official coalition which acts as the guardian and publisher of exemplary catholic and reformed models, and in the manifold wisdom of the Kirk fringe, where a dispersed commonwealth of practitioners explore the common and uncommon goods of worship. The future of worship in the Church of Scotland requires both and belongs to both.

Notes

1 This text has been lightly edited, and the style still reflects its origins as a lecture, given in the Parish Church of St Cuthbert, Edinburgh, on 23 May 2010.

2 Howard G. Hageman, 'Three Lectures', in Gregg Mast (ed.), *In Remembrance and Hope: The Ministry and Vision of Howard G. Hageman* (Grand Rapids: Eerdmans, 1998).

3 Margo Todd, *The Culture of Protestantism in Early Modern Scotland* (New Haven, CT: Yale University Press, 2002), p. 108.

4 Even through these changes, it remains the term we are looking for.

5 I quote this as someone who is identified with a broad evangelical position.

6 Patrick Malloy, *Celebrating the Eucharist* (New York: Church Publishing, 2007), pp. 16–17.

7 Frank Birch Brown, *Good Taste, Bad Taste, and Christian Taste: Aesthetics in Religious Life* (Oxford: Oxford University Press, 2000), and *Inclusive Yet Discerning: Navigating Worship Artfully*, the Calvin Institute of Christian Worship Liturgical Studies (Grand Rapids: Eerdmans, 2009).

8 I heard a well-respected conservative evangelical, linked to the Crieff Fellowship, talk about having undertaken further postgraduate study (a DMin or such) through a conservative Reformed seminary in North America. He was quite candid about how study around worship and the sacraments had given him a new awareness of how a more classically structured, responsive liturgy might be more authentically reformed than the rather pared down neo-baptist version he had been extemporising around. The cultural issues in play – a desire to distance themselves from High Church formalism and from a more theologically liberal

stance among some Scoto-Catholics – have promoted a particularly low style of communion liturgy among conservative evangelicals in Scotland, which may not be well integrated with their self-understanding of themselves as 'reformed'?

9 Mr Still had encouraged people to take on this challenge, but lesser minds and hearts have not often done so..

10 Pete Ward, *Selling Worship* (Milton Keynes: Paternoster, 2005).

11 D. Forrester and D. Gay (eds), *Worship and Liturgy in Context* (London: SCM, 2009).

12 See the early essay on embodied worship by Stephen Winward in Ronald Jasper (ed.), *The Renewal of Worship* (Oxford: OUP, 1965) and the discussion in Doug Gay, *Remixing the Church* (London: SCM, 2011).

ASSIST OUR SONG

Theological perspectives on worship and its music

DOUGLAS GALBRAITH

Given at the 2010 Annual Meeting of the Church Service Society[1]

Introduction

The invitation from the Chalmers Trustees to contribute to this group of lectures to mark the 450th anniversary of the Scottish Reformation proposed a liturgical dimension, observing (with reference to the original purpose of the Trust to uphold 'the Headship of Christ over His Church') that 'contemporary worship, when it fails to meet the highest-quality standards, sometimes does so because it fails to acknowledge the Divine sovereignty, or it lapses into something more akin to entertainment of the congregation'. What, however, are these 'highest-quality standards'? Indeed, should we be seeking objective standards at all by which to measure an act of worship, or does its efficacy – if that is a word we can use – lie beyond human measure? In the early 1990s, as Visiting Scholar in a theological college in Adelaide, I was seconded to a group of congregations for a month to partner them in reviewing and developing their worship. During an incognito (I thought) reconnaissance visit the Sunday before, I was spotted by the lay preacher, who gave me a rather guarded welcome while reassuring the congregation, with a meaningful glance in my direction: 'The Lord doesn't look for quality in worship; He looks for effort'!

There is a sense abroad of a need for an assessment of contemporary trends in worship, whether these are driven by liturgical renewal, by ecumenical convergence or by mission initiatives like 'emerging church' or 'fresh expressions'. Several proposals have been made; and some are referred to below. These have tended to stay close to the shape and intention of the liturgy or to the 'house rules' of the various media of worship, be they drama, music, the visual arts and so on. In this paper, an attempt is made to go further back, to first principles as articulated in the aims of the lectureship (modified after the Union of 1929 to 'the general doctrine of the Church and kingdom of Christ, or any subject cognate thereto') – to a Church, in the words of the Scottish Reformers, whose 'true notes' are always to be measured against 'the Word of God, in which God has revealed himself to us'.[2] It seeks an ecclesiological basis for a critique that can be applied to the various worship practices adopted in the present day – that is, to the several 'media' through which worship takes place. Given that the material of this paper draws particularly on research undertaken in the area of theology and church music, there will be a bias towards that medium; but it is hoped that, where a more general application is not expressly indicated, the reader will readily be able to make the connection.[3]

Drivers of change

That many, particularly in the 'mainstream' branches of the Church, view these trends as worrying is evident, lamenting (as they see it) a looseness of language, ritual compromised by informality, and disturbance caused by technology. They may also feel alienated by a casualness of liturgical dress, an absence of intellectual challenge, the intrusion of personality into presidency, and music which does not match the import of the event. These reactions are not against one particular style of worship; they may be provoked as much by the work of mainline liturgical

A coup by the Assembly of the United Reformed Church (Edinburgh 2008) when three leading hymn writers were brought together: (*left to right*) Alan Gaunt, Brian Wren, Fred Kaan, with interviewer Stephen Brown.

© Mark Howard, Twenty-Five Educational

commissions as by imports from other traditions or cultures. Since it is not always possible for people to exercise choice and go elsewhere, local equilibrium can be disturbed. As the American commentator Frank Burch Brown ruefully observes: 'Few things at present create more persistent conflict within Christian congregations than differences over worship style, music and media (especially "contemporary" versus "traditional")'.[4] There are echoes of this in the somewhat despairing ring of the titles of many contemporary publications about church music:

> *Why Catholics Can't Sing: The Culture of Catholicism and the Triumph of Bad Taste*;[5]
>
> *Reaching Out Without Dumbing Down*;[6]
>
> *Good Taste, Bad Taste and Christian Taste*;[7]

Weary and Ill at Ease (reporting an English survey of clergy and organists);[8] and
'It may be refreshing – but is it reformed?'[9]

For clearer analysis, it is necessary to distinguish between the different motivations which lie behind changes that have taken, and are taking, place. In the documents of Vatican II, the emphasis was on enabling the people (the 'assembly') to participate more fully in worship and in a way that affirmed and echoed their cultural context (although more recent revisions of the Mass text in English are seen by many as taking a step back from this position). For denominations where participation was already (at least theoretically) the norm, revision of liturgical materials have sought language, imagery and forms which have better contemporary resonance and which truly express the prayers of the times.

Another driver of change, in an increasingly secular and pluralist age in which churches struggle to keep the ear of the population, is the wish to release the mission dimension of worship. This has given rise to initiatives which find fresh materials for worship within the culture of the time, including the most advanced means of communication which have been developed, and which by these 'alternative' forms have succeeded in gathering together many who might have been untouched by traditional procedures. Such initiatives, at their best, can both reach further into the culture and into the heart of liturgy and can have a renewing function in both directions.[10] Other manifestations, however, such as the group of styles which have become known as 'seeker-sensitive' worship, have been criticised for their too-ready alliance with the spirit of the age and for their propensity for simply omitting anything which might alienate by its strangeness, or which assumes too much knowledge, or which might demand too much effort. One prescription, for what is described as the Next Church, lays down that there must be:

> No spires. No crosses. No robes. No clerical collars. No hard pews. No kneelers. No biblical gobbledygook. No prayerly rote. No fire. No brimstone. No pipe organs. No dreary eighteenth-century hymns. No forced solemnity. No Sunday finery. No collection plates.[11]

When so much is omitted, what fills the gaps? The answer is a greater focus on the 'platform', where the leaders need to win and retain the attention of those who are sometimes referred to as 'worship guests'. The strong element of performance, by charismatic speaker, by highly professional singers and band, even the building and its environment of such appointments as swimming pools or gardens, as well as keeping people coming, help forge a loyalty to the 'brand', the frequently independent organisation whose governance structure is akin to a successful business company. Such corporate 'ministries' may use the language of the consumerist culture, for example in the manner in which it targets its clientele: 'Whether a church uses contemporary music or not defines which kind of people it wants'.[12] American Lutheran Gordon Lathrop asks[13] whether the kind of participation that results bears sufficient relation to what true participation in worship and discipleship must consist in:

> Can Christian faith be reduced to an idea, without the body of the Bible, communally read, sung and preached, and without the body of the sacraments? Will not the very manner of the seeker service, with its studied attempt to make no demands upon the audience, communicate a Christianity without assembly, a Christianity that has become only an individually useful commodity? In fact, can the gospel be authentically presented without the assembly?

The last references have been North American, but there is plenty of evidence that these developments do not relate to any one geographical location or set of circumstances. Styles of music and worship are infectious and have a short incubation time. Frank Burch Brown expresses concern at the way what he dubs the easy-listening 'lounge-style' music of the megachurches, used to embrace seekers, very quickly has become the idiom of choice for 'finders' – that is, many in the mainstream churches.[14] The Protestant commentator Edward Farley memorably captured the effect on many congregations of a loss, as he and many others see it, of transcendence and dignity in worship, when he wrote:

> To attend the typical Protestant Sunday morning worship service is to experience something odd, something like a charade. ... Lacking is a sense of the terrible mystery of God, which sets language atremble and silences facile chattiness. ... If the seraphim assumed this Sunday morning mood, they would be addressing God not as 'holy, holy, holy' but as 'nice, nice, nice'.[15]

Let us emphasise at this point that the tensions, when properly understood, are not between the 'traditional' and the 'contemporary'. The term 'tradition' is often used dismissively to mean a surviving outward manner whose original power has been lost. Our worship traditions, however, do not hand on 'the remains of the day' so much as capture a constantly unfolding and living encounter with God, to which people have brought the best of their gifts, and of which we today are an evolving part. Indeed, tradition, as John Zizioulas reminds us, does not just bring the past and the present into relationship but also places both in relation to the Parousia: 'The true criterion of Tradition is ... to be found in the revelation of what the world will be like in the kingdom'.[16] If anything encourages continuing work on 'getting the liturgy right',[17] the idea that we have still to uncover the fullness of our traditions surely does.

Worship, then, is not so much a 'form' (e.g. 'traditional', 'contemporary', 'experimental', 'alternative') as a *flow*; and, when we look for 'quality', what we seek, in part, is a gauge which measures how far each newest expression emerges from the worship whose shape through the ages has been wrought from the mix of attention to Scripture, reception of tradition and the human encounter with the mystery of God, through the grace and challenge of the Holy Spirit. In talking of standards, one of our questions is: how do we make sure that

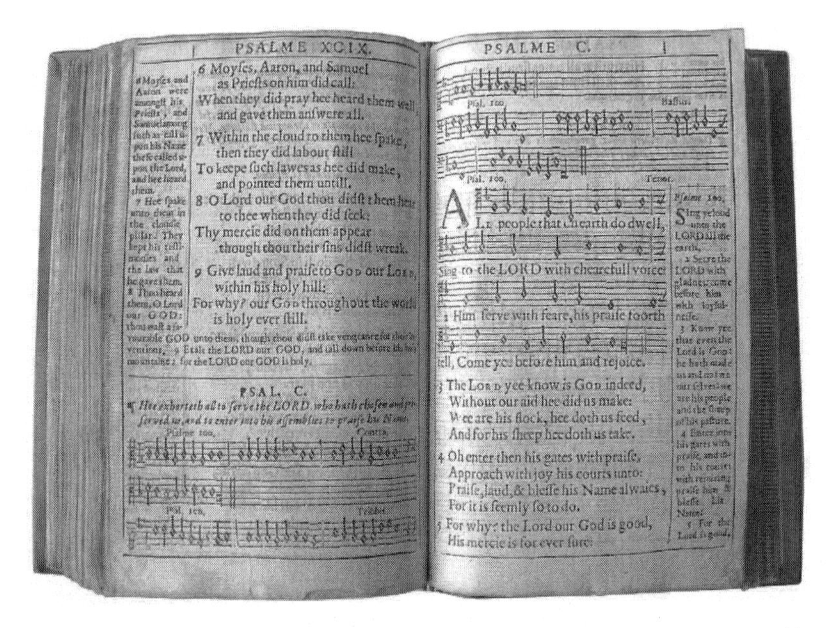
PSALME XCIX.

6 Moyſes, Aaron, and Samuel
as Prieſts on him did call:
When they did pray hee heard them well
and gave them anſwere all.

7 Within the cloud to them hee ſpake,
then they did labour ſtill
To keepe ſuch lawes as hee did make,
and pointed them untill.

8 O Lord our God thou didſt them hear
to thee when they did ſeek:
Thy mercie did on them appear
though thou their ſins didſt wreak.

9 Give laud and praiſe to GOD our LORD,
within his holy hill:
For why? our GOD throughout the world
is holy ever ſtill.

PSAL. C.

PSALME C.

ALL people that on earth do dwell,
Sing to the LORD with chearefull voice:
2 Him ſerve with feare, his praiſe foorth tell,
Come yee before him and rejoice.

3 The LORD yee know is GOD indeed,
Without our aid hee did us make:
Wee are his flock, hee doth us feed,
And for his ſheep hee doth us take.

4 Oh enter then his gates with praiſe,
Approach with joy his courts unto:
Praiſe, laud, & bleſſe his Name alwaies,
For it is ſeemly ſo to do.

5 For why? the Lord our God is good,
His mercie is for ever ſure:

A key Reformation principle was the full participation of the congregation in worship. *The Forme of Prayers* from 1564 onwards (also referred to as 'Knox's Liturgy' or 'The Book of Common Order') provided the Psalms with tunes to enable this. Later editions printed all four parts so that they could be sung in harmony. This shows Psalm 100 from the 1635 edition.

Photo: Peter Forrest

current practice is enriched by what has been handed down, while at the same time finding tradition renewed and continued? It is often when we 'search our traditions', all the while open to God's future, that we find the best ideas for the fuller worship that we seek. An earlier initiative on this basis was *New Ways to Worship* (1980), nearly all of whose authors were members – indeed past or future presidents – of this Society,[18] a book multiple copies of which are now finding their way back to the maternal bosom via the Edinburgh Christian Aid book sale!

The Church Service Society and the contemporary debate

From its founding in 1865, the Church Service Society has addressed matters relating to contemporary worship practice, coupling this with the study of historic liturgies. Recent years have been no exception. Three further factors which impinge on this discussion have already been identified and explored in addresses given to this Society or in publications by members. These are: overload on worship; the effect of technological advance; and the consumerist culture of the time.

Overloading weekly worship

Several writers identify the effect on worship of the multiple social allegiances of our contemporaries and the resultant telescoping of what would within living memory have been a whole week's church life into one hour on Sunday morning. This issues in a more complex event, which may try to combine the creation *de novo* of a sense of community, welcome to the stranger, the development of the individual life of the spirit, affirmation of culture and context, full participation, outreach to the enquirer, and a sense of connection with the communion of saints, while all the time seeking to open the way to a recognition of, and encounter with, the beyond-in-the-midst. This was among the aspects of modern worship discussed by Canon Michael Perham, since 2004 Bishop of Gloucester, addressing the Society in 1995. Worship was 'about nothing less than putting us in touch with the reality of

God'. For this to occur, a new prayerfulness was required, 'a kind of undercurrent that gives quality and authenticity to everything else'.[19] In that direction lies true participation.

Technology and worship

Professor John R. Hume, in a paper given to the Society in May 2007, demonstrated how many were the things we now take for granted that were made possible by advances in technology. In addition to the size and scope of the pipe organ, he listed (among other things) construction techniques which enabled larger buildings; glass-making and painting providing a way of teaching and a focus for worship; mechanical methods of sawing timber making larger roofs possible; cast-iron columns instead of stone pillars enabling galleries and improved sightlines; lighting; the making of paper and printing; heating for greater comfort; amplification. Hume called for experimentation and a critical openness to new technologies, but always measured against the essence of worship:

> We should always aspire to the first-rate, for only in that can we worship God in spirit and in truth. We should also be conscious of the importance of dignity, integrity and authenticity in worship. In apparently trivialising, in over-simplifying, in using the artificial rather than the real, we demean the act of worship, and debase the relationship between the worshipping community and the Divine.[20]

Consumers of worship

The third issue, that belief in God and the worship of God is increasingly a matter for consumer choice, has been newly addressed in the book, *The Worship Mall*, by a past president of the Church Service Society, Professor Bryan Spinks of Yale.[21] This is a description and analysis of the wide array of styles of worship practised today. The metaphor of the mall suggests

A unique event when in 2009 Pluscarden Abbey hosted a Symposium on Scottish sacred music, involving representatives from churches and universities, together with choirs and other performers. The gathering is here addressed by the Abbot, Fr Hugh Gilbert, now RC Bishop of Aberdeen.

Photo © Martin Gardner

that worship competes with other commodities in offering satisfaction; worship events are 'successful' insofar as they provide the satisfaction that is sought rather than for other characteristics (like historical authenticity, theological integrity or ecclesiastical authority). Spinks, noting that worship is at the same time incarnational and incultured, warns that too often the balance is not achieved and that Christian worship can be reduced to a 'cultural incantation'.[22]

Recalling the assertion of the Dominican liturgical scholar Aidan Kavanagh that '(i)nculturation ... is a precious mystery in itself of which God is the agent' (cf. the 'divine sovereignty' of the Chalmers prescription, above), in the face of the many attempts he describes to find an appropriate style of worship for contemporary culture, Spinks concludes that the 'organic development of liturgy, *providing the liturgical tradition is open to change*, will probably be more successful than liturgical genetic engineering where we are always intervening to *make* the liturgy contemporary'.[23]

Some proposals for evaluation

From all sides, there are attempts to regulate the situation and to provide markers. These were brought together by the international academic body, *Societas Liturgica*, at Turku in Finland in 1997, when scholars and liturgical practitioners from across the world engaged with the issues as they affected the Church's music. From the Roman Catholic side, where the debate has been conducted with the greatest urgency, the principal criteria were those derived from music's liturgical function.[24] The question to be put regarding music written or proposed for liturgical use was how adequately it satisfied the demands of the liturgy itself. In her presidential address, Professor Irmgard Pahl sought 'critical criteria of a qualitative nature' when aspects of the liturgical action would lend their characteristics to its music, such as the incarnational nature of the Word (expressing both the conditionedness and the creative potential of humanity), liturgy's doxological intent, its festive quality – seven in all, and all indicative as to where music might find its best and fullest expression for worship.[25]

This approach, building on the Vatican II definition that music is 'a necessary and integral part of the solemn liturgy', is by no means exclusively Catholic. United Methodist Don Saliers bases his critique on the notion of 'sung prayer' – that is, the corporate prayer of the liturgy[26] – while John Witvliet of the Calvin Institute of Christian Worship in Michigan speaks of the need for 'liturgical discernment'.[27] Nearer home, in two magisterial papers on church music, one of which was the Lee

Lecture of 1964, and both published in the Society's *Annual*,[28] the late Stewart Todd, a former president of the Society, developed the idea of music as handmaid of worship, with the greatest danger being when music became 'too musical', got above itself and thus failed to serve. However, alert to the possible criticism that this was too narrowly functional a reading of the place of music, he balances this by saying that 'it is not so much the dignity of the task that ennobles the servant as the dignity of the Lord the servant serves'.

This starting point for evaluation, that liturgy should be the measure of music, can be – and has been – criticised as bestowing a finality on liturgy, seeing it as a perfect expression of the Church, a construct which has authority over other aspects of Christian utterance. Experience in faith-and-order studies when liturgy is approached as raw material for dialogue[29] is that *lex orandi* can raise as many problems as it clarifies. There is also the difficulty that the privileging of liturgy as a whole over its media renders it impossible for these media, including music, to be seen as possible change agents. Difficulties such as these have led the Catholic bishops of the USA, in one of many contributions offered in elucidation of the prescriptions of Vatican II, to posit a broader, threefold basis for critique, namely that evaluation of musical settings should consist of musical, pastoral and liturgical dimensions, all of equal importance but at the same time seen as one.[30]

First, music should be subject to the *rules of music*, drawing on the areas of musicology and aesthetics. Second, the music must connect culturally with the *assembly*, taking into account those for whom it is composed and their circumstances, capable of uniting the worshippers and enabling them to express themselves musically. Finally, the music must be a sufficient partner to the *liturgy* in terms of appropriateness, depth and meaning. This promisingly comprehensive approach did not, however, find universal acceptance. Would each dimension not tend to cancel others out and lead back to where we started? Alternatively, with the stipulation that these were not three separate criteria but one composite one, how much authority could be given to each, not least the music?[31] The debate continues, and some have seen the need to go 'further back' and find criteria for evaluation beyond the liturgical context.

An approach through ecclesiology

The possibility that worship and its media might be regulated by our understanding of the Church itself has already been explored by the noted commentator on church music, Erik Routley. Two books, one at the beginning of his career, the other towards the end – similar, but modified after a lifetime of reflection[32] – sought scriptural principles to apply to church-music criticism, including the image of the Church as the body of Christ. While these were not systematic treatments of that image, they have been suggestive to later researchers, including the present writer.

While faith-and-order discussion around the 'body of Christ', at its height in the 1950s and 1960s, is by no means exhausted, its place has been taken in recent decades by the image of *koinonia* (Latin *communio*), the lens currently used by churches in dialogue and multilateral discussion, valued for its ability to bring into focus an understanding of the church that resonates both with Scripture and with the traditions represented by its mainstream expressions. How may we extract from an image like this a toolkit for the assessment of contemporary initiatives in worship, including music? My own reading of bilateral and multilateral discussion, together with World Council of Churches Faith and Order Papers, has resulted in the identification of five aspects or dimensions of this image which potentially could offer more focused tools. It is not possible in the space given here to examine all of these; one only is developed here to indicate how the process

Participants at the World Council of Churches Assembly, Porto Alegre, Brazil in 2006 whose document *Called to be the One Church* developed further the dimensions within *koinonia*.

Photo: (United Methodist Youth Services) Paulino Menezes, WCC

might be applied, while the others are summarised. Together, they are capable both of addressing the 'economy' of music-making in the church (its organisation and 'delivery') as well as the detail of the music itself (the latter a more controversial suggestion). It is important at this point to note that, in this discussion, the focus is not on the words that are set so much as on the music itself, acknowledging that there will be compositions where it is impossible to assess the music separately, where text and music combine to make a 'new creation'.

Study of these sources suggests that *koinonia* is understood as a *sacramental* community, a *relational* community, a *diaconal* community, a *diverse* community and a community growing towards *maturity in Christ*. The first of these dimensions is selected for closer examination.

A sacramental community

Koinonia and related forms occur thirty-six times in the New Testament. A key passage is in 1 Corinthians 10, where an identification is made between the body of Christ – the community at Corinth – and the crucified body of Christ, proclaimed in the sharing of bread and wine. This bestows upon the former a unique quality that sets it apart from any known model of human gathering. When Paul returns to this theme, as often, he uses the term 'member' to describe the relationship not between individual participants and an organisation, but between the *koinonia* and Christ, thus defining the source of its life.[33] That is, when this community gathers, it gathers with Christ, whose presence is affirmed anew in the Eucharist, its prayers patterned on Christ's own and prompted by the Holy Spirit, the active energy which both gives the assembly its unique identity and initiates its worship. This is echoed in the final report of the Reformed–Roman Catholic dialogue which took place between 1970 and 1977, *The Presence of Christ in Church and World*, when, in a substantial section, it is acknowledged that 'the concept of *koinonia* stresses not only fellowship with the exalted Lord Jesus Christ, but beyond this and precisely because of this also the fellowship of all who partake of the meal and are called together into the community of the Lord'.[34]

What kind of music conforms to this intimacy between Church and Christ? Negatively, there is music which can arrest the body of Christ at the level of a purely human gathering. It may do no more than promote human solidarity, albeit Christian solidarity. This is music whose initial effect on the hearers is to make them feel satisfaction in their communal life, confirming people in their own interpretation of themselves without trying to draw them forward from their comfort zones. The corollary may be that it inhibits the ability of the worshipper to capture a sense of the numinous.

Koinonia as a sacramental community. The comprehensive survey currently taking place throughout the Church of Scotland is recording all Communion vessels which belong to local congregations, while also encouraging churches to make use of these historic symbols.

Photo © Kirkpatrick Dobie

It is important, given the debate in the churches today, to say at this point that a judgement is not being made on particular styles or idioms of music and their suitability for liturgical use. Here too, a 'mixed economy' can be appropriate. Rather, a critique is being offered to help establish whether the music employed in the liturgy is 'all that music can be'. Musicologists like Victor Zuckerkandl, in seeking the essence of music, employ the term 'transcendence'. Rejecting the divide between material and spiritual, he contrasts the world of the person and the world to which the person relates. These two 'worlds' are not over against each other but within each other; and music enables access to the depth of both. This kind of assessment can be applied to music and found present whether it is a Byrd mass, a Genevan psalm tune or, say, 'Summertime' from *Porgy and Bess*.

The music that is part of our liturgy must be capable of such boundary-crossing. It may warmly embrace, but at the same time it must be such as leaves room for Christ to move freely among those who make up the body. It is music capable of directing our thoughts through and beyond our belonging together to our being one in Christ; music which has a numinous or transcendent quality at the same time as recognising our need for each other; music which – after, within or in spite of the human contribution that has been made – mediates the divine.

One way of isolating the qualities which make music acceptable for this purpose is to examine forms which have been experienced over a length of time as being effective in enabling the presence of Christ to be recognised and palpable, forms such as plainsong, or Anglican chant, or the metrical psalm tune, or polyphony, or the Lutheran chorale. It would take too much space to examine each in turn for their different qualities – but, in general, one might instance the spaces within the music, the modesty of movement, the resting places, the repetitions, the lightness of touch, the diverting of attention towards the words or the rituals, which give room for the soul to gaze or to feel gazed upon, as if by an icon.[35] There is a 'right-sizedness' about these musical forms, which is Nathan Mitchell's definition of reverence,[36] a definition which can embrace both dignity and silence as much as the exuberance and rhythmic interest.

Lest this reference to well-tried liturgical forms suggest that only such music is capable of unveiling the beyond-in-the-midst, it must be affirmed that the measurements being proposed may be applied to any music written for or used within worship. All of the forms mentioned above have everyday music in their family tree, some of them being direct descendants (it is best to avoid the use of 'popular' in this context, since the term meant different things in different ages), although all, through time or compositional processes or happy union with liturgical texts, have become able to open the minds and hearts of those gathered for worship. Time and use will apply this measure to more popular styles used in worship today, but it may also be possible to critique contemporary worship music and to winnow out now what would in the end be unlikely to survive, and thus help to avoid offering disappointing and unfulfilling experiences of worship to people of our time – experiences which, for example, contribute to a falling-away after initial enthusiasm, or becoming disillusioned with the faith because of confinement within a particular expression of worship or a particular group of people when the music fails to point a way through.

With regard to musical composition, a proper test of applying the measurement to music itself requires several examples; and there is danger in offering just two. Yet this may provide a taste, or at least give an illustration, as to how each of the five aspects, while all have their more general application, may also act as aural instruments for the examination of sequences of notes and harmonic progressions. The song 'Bind us together' is now established in the repertoire; it is also popular at weddings. It consists of a refrain,

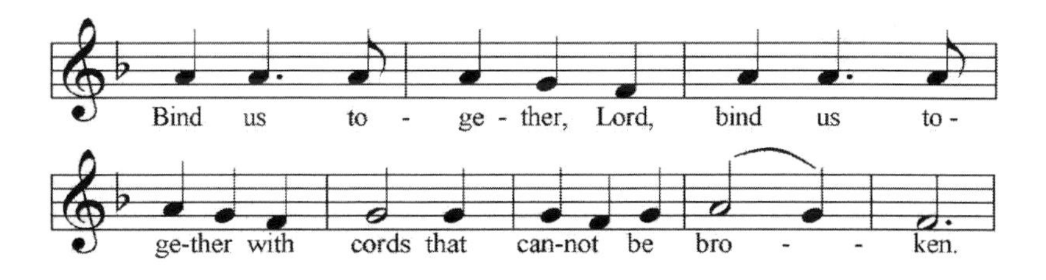

using three notes only, all moving by step. This in itself is not an issue when one thinks of what plainchant can express in few notes and small intervals between them; but the repetitive nature of their arrangement does not contribute to a feeling of movement. This is compounded by the fact that each phrase returns downward to the lowest note, the 'tonic' and 'home-base' of the melody, suggesting rest and closure as opposed to seeking and receptivity. The feeling is of the melody circling round within itself, which somehow doesn't encourage the lifting of the spiritual gaze. The whole phrase is then repeated with a slight alteration at the end, serving perhaps to reinforce the impression given by the first part. The prayer to 'bind us together' may be answered, but are we merely feeling good together rather than being lifted into a 'new creation' in Christ? However, there is always the chance that the middle section will offer an opening. It runs:

Although it begins on a new, higher, note, the end harks back to the refrain, and the repeat is exact. There is thus throughout the song an atmosphere of stasis, of never moving away from where we started. There is no room for the unexpected.

The second example is also from a 'popular' style of song. It is a folk tune dating back at least to the eighteenth century, when it was known to the text 'Oh, the shearin's no' for me'. The better-known nineteenth-century text was 'Let us haste to Kelvin Grove, bonnie lassie, O' – and the melody is now popular to the modern Christian text 'Will you come and follow me?'[37] The structure consists of a first line of melody, repeated almost exactly but with a modified ending. A new middle section is followed by a repetition of the original idea. The melody begins by moving step by step, in an upward and then a downward direction. This small detail in itself offers the feeling of anticipation, which is even more marked with the rising leap at the end of the phrase (a):

This is also present in the second line, a smaller leap (b), but one which betrays the origins of the musical style in which this melody is written. Although it does make an appearance in the third bar, missing virtually throughout the melody is the 'leading note', 'ti' in the sol-fa scale, the note that leads to the tonic, the home-base of the melody. The melody thus echoes those earlier folk melodies which use the 'gapped scale'. Indeed, the opening phrase mimics the simplest form of this, the pentatonic scale, a scale of five notes, with two gaps, common in the folk song of many cultures.[38]

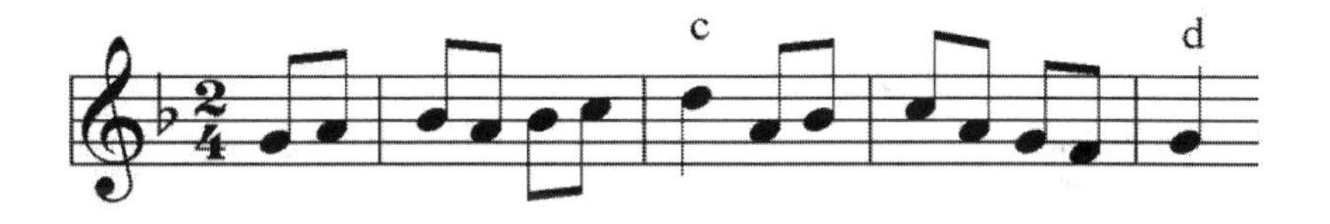

The middle section opens with a phrase which, perhaps significantly, ends with what would be the top, and remotest, note of the pentatonic scale (c). Although we are considering the melody, we are conscious of its harmonic implications and may have the sense here of having moved to another key. This feeling of 'moving outside' is continued as the melody moves to a semi-closure in what is felt to be a further key (d), the dominant, which acts as a springboard to 'return' to the first key and indeed melody. There is thus a sense of movement and exploration, with points of expectation – a sense, if you like, of a 'beyond'.

Much folk song has in common with plainsong the 'church modes', with their shifting feeling of 'home' and 'away' (all eight are found in Scottish folk song, even the rare Lydian mode, an example of which is used in *Common Ground*).[39] Like plainsong also, folk song is typically performed by unaccompanied voices. This common modal foundation may enable much folk song to share the characteristic of being 'revisitable' – with gaps still to be filled, the utterance never complete, moments of the unexpected which 'lift the curtain' into the numinous.

There is another reason why the folk idiom may be eloquent in worship. At first sight, folk songs seem to be very much attached to 'the world'. Their themes celebrate humanity and the structures of human life, but there is characteristically the acknowledgement of certain realities – of death, of loss of love, of the hardship of survival. Folk song serves to bind people into community or into a common task. It brings people together in humanity, not just in a particular corner of humanity but humanity as a whole. It is folk song which is often a country's most readily exportable commodity. But it also has the capacity of being open to larger questions. It has deeply unifying undertones: its subject matter tends to chronicle the unreliability of human relationships, of the reality of violence, of the inevitability of death. But it does so with text often polished by centuries of repetition. Its music matches this: the melodies have that tinge of dissent, melancholy, resignation which suggests powers outwith the realm of human responsibility, a touch of the transcendent. Perhaps it is these hints of otherness which haunt folk song that have caused hymn-book editors from Ralph Vaughan Williams[40] onwards to find in examples of this genre music which seems so at home in the church and its worship, inviting us to reflect not just on these human themes but on the Word made flesh, dwelling among us.

The General Assembly of the Church of Scotland in session, an expression of the relational dimension of *koinonia*, being addressed by the Archbishop of Canterbury, Rowan Williams.

© Church of Scotland

Other aspects of koinonia

Each of the other four aspects may be developed in a similar way to the above. They will variously be found to address different dimensions of music and music-making.

The *relational* aspect, building on the mutuality patterned on the perichoresis of the three persons of the Trinity, calls in question any elitism and affirms that the church's doxology is contributed to by persons in multiple roles of equal importance who relate to each other in a texture of belonging and mutual accounting. Such a relationship is found to be also endemic in the music. In its music-making, the church is helped to discover its true nature as a body where relationship is not happened upon but given as gift. The growing recovery of antiphonal and other participative styles is part of this awareness.

The *diaconal* dimension reveals the kernel of service that lies at the heart of church and gospel, which engages with broken community and strains towards the coming reconciliation of all things with their Creator. Doxology, thanksgiving and communion offer a 'sign, instrument and foretaste' of the Kingdom. Music can fail to serve when it declares dominating allegiances, or asserts cultural priorities, or displays personal idiosyncrasies. However, recent biblical and cultural study of the concept does not support a secondary or lowlier role for music but suggests rather a 'go-between' function.[41] Thus it

Symbols of service (*diakonia*) at the monthly Holy City event in Glasgow hosted by the Iona Community, 'a rendezvous of faithful folk, curious enquirers and compelling doubters, drawn from the whole ... spectrum of Christian traditions, their edges and beyond'. Each evening consists of 'participative, reflective workshops ... (and) liturgy engaging body, mind and spirit'.

Photo: Jo Love

Koinonia as growing into Christ – spiritual maturity. Circular prayer area in Old St Paul's Episcopal Church and labyrinth beyond to mirror and shape the journey of faith, created by Carol Marples of Soul Marks Trust for the official Edinburgh Hogmanay celebration 2012–13.

© *Carol Marples*

must be music in its fullest sense, which uses all its art in the service of the Kingdom. It is an aspect, also, which challenges the quality of service between different musical groups and that rendered by musician to musician.

The *diverse* nature of *koinonia*, seen as something given ('we, who are many, are one body in Christ, and … members one of another' – Romans 12:5) rather than a problem to be solved, suggests a source of enrichment for the church's music, but there is a point at which diversity can become destructive to the community. 'Blended' worship may not be the solution it seems. Gordon Lathrop's categories (in terms, for example, of images, music and the remembrance of the saints) of the 'local' and 'more-than-local', and the proposal that where the former was present so should be the latter, may be helpful. This can be expressed through a mixture of idiom in a composition, or a different arrangement for a melody, or by careful juxtapositioning of styles.

The nature of *koinonia* as a community growing towards *maturity in Christ* challenges the music that is written and selected as well as all those who make it. With baptism seen as a process towards sanctification and justification (1 Corinthians 6:11), music must further rather than inhibit this. The subtle and varied vocabulary of music is well equipped to foster growth. Mode and modulation, metre that spans a phrase or a whole movement, the interplay of strands and voices, repetition and contrast, shape and structure, all carry the listener forward not just to the end of the piece but beyond. Yet much music written for worship contains no sense of journeying or searching. An idea may be given but is merely repeated rather than developed; or, written in one key, it fails to notice the opportunities to explore adjacent keys with their feeling of moving beyond and returning. Such

Koinonia and diversity. A 'big band' sound is added to the resources for contemporary worship. The band was formed by Rev Dr Robin Hill (centre left, alto saxophone) and is conducted by Richard Michael (front, with flute). The venue is St Cuthbert's Church, Edinburgh, during the Heart & Soul event of 2013.

© Willie Ewan

music may trap us at a level of immaturity, however safe and satisfying.

Conclusion

One possible advantage of such ecclesiologically based criteria is that they are bedded in the experience of being in the church and are potentially useable by the people of the church generally rather than only by the 'theologically literate' or the professional artist/musician. It may therefore be possible to develop from this a *common discourse* through which worship committees, clergy-musician planning meetings and church members in conversation might achieve greater understanding of each other's positions. It is possible that such a mode of discourse, if developed, could be found relevant also to other areas of controversy in the church where professional approaches are found to clash with popular opinion, such as in matters concerned with the reordering of the sanctuary.

This would mean encouraging more conscious reflection on people's experience of being in the church, as well as on their knowledge of worship through long participation, together with their natural human ability as musicians and artists. Such a dialogue, with its starting point in what people already 'know', would be preferable to criteria applied by outside authority. Members of Christ already know Christ's presence in communion, have found themselves changed as they reach in relationship to each other, have been challenged and renewed by costly service, have struggled with the diversity in their own community and in human society, and long for the increase in love and spiritual insight that accompanies a growth to maturity in Christ. They are well on the way to being equipped to evaluate the worship in which they engage and the music and the other media through which it is expressed, all in the interests of the fullest experience of worship.

Notes

1 The lecture was also given as the 2010 Presidential Address to the Church Service Society on Thursday, 26 May 2010. The main title is from Richard Baxter's hymn 'Ye holy angels bright' (*Church Hymnary* 4, no. 179).

2 'The notes of the true Kirk, therefore, we believe, confess, and avow to be: first, the true preaching of the Word of God, in which God has revealed himself to us, as the writings of the prophets and apostles declare; secondly, the right administration of the sacraments of Christ Jesus, with which must be associated the Word and promise of God to seal and confirm them in our hearts; and lastly, ecclesiastical discipline uprightly ministered, as God's Word prescribes, whereby vice is repressed and virtue nourished' *The Confession of Faith* 1560 (the '*Scots Confession*') (chapter 18).

3 The part of the lecture which deals with music is drawn from research undertaken in the area of church music and theology through the International Centre for Sacred Music Studies, Bangor University. I am grateful to Professor John Harper of the School of Music at Bangor, and at that time also Director General of the Royal School of Church Music, my principal supervisor, and to the Revd Dr Robert Pope of the School of Religious Studies, a minister of the United Reformed Church.

4 Frank Burch Brown, *Good Taste, Bad Taste and Christian Taste: Aesthetics in Religious Life* (Oxford: Oxford University Press, 2000), chapter 1.

5 Thomas Day (Crossroad, 1991).

6 Marva Dawn, *Reaching Out Without Dumbing Down: A Theology of Worship for the Turn-of-the-Century Church* (Grand Rapids: Eerdmans, 1995).

7 See note 4 above.

8 Robin Rees, *Weary and Ill at Ease: A Survey of Clergy and Organists* (Leominster: Gracewing, 1993). The reference is to the poem 'The lost chord', beginning 'Seated one day at the organ', by Adelaide Anne Procter (1858), and set to music by Arthur Sullivan in 1877.

9 Title of paper by D. G. Hart in *Calvin Theological Journal* 32:2 (November 1997), pp. 407–22.

10 See, for example, Jonny Baker, *Curating Worship* (London: SPCK, 2010), and J. Baker, D. Gay and J. Brown, *Alternative Worship* (London: SPCK, 2003). But note Bryan Spinks' remarks on inculturation, below, section 3.

11 Charles Trueheart, 'Welcome to the next church', *The Atlantic Online*, www.theatlantic.com/issues/96aug/nxtchrch/nxtchrch.htm.

12 Loc. cit.

13 Gordon Lathrop, *Holy People: A Liturgical Ecclesiology* (Minneapolis: Fortress Press, 1999), p. 92.

14 Frank Burch Brown, 'Religious meanings and musical styles: a matter of taste?', in Charlotte Kroeker (ed.), *Music in Christian Worship* (Collegeville: Liturgical Press, 2005), pp. 141–2.

15 Edward Farley, 'A missing presence', *Christian Century* (18–25 March 1998), p. 276. Also http://findarticles.com/p/articles/mi_m1058/is_n9_v115/ai_20460250/.

16 John Zizioulas, 'The church as communion', in Best and Gassman (eds), *On the Way to Fuller Koinonia*, Faith and Order Paper 166 (Geneva: WCC Publications, 1994), pp. 103–11.

17 *Getting the Liturgy Right* was a volume published by the Joint Liturgical Group to which Stewart Todd, the then current President, and James Stewart, a future President, of the Church Service Society, contributed.

18 Published by Saint Andrew Press for the Church of Scotland's Committee on Public Worship and Aids to Devotion.

19 *The Record* of the Church Service Society, vol. 31 (1996), p. 5.

20 John R. Hume, *The Record* of the Church Service Society, vol. 43 (2007–8), p. 23.

21 Bryan D. Spinks, *The Worship Mall: Contemporary Responses to Contemporary Culture*, Alcuin Club Collections 85 (London: SPCK, 2010). This formed the basis for the Society's Study Conference at Cumbrae in September 2010. It was reviewed by Rachel Dobie in *The Record* of the Church Service Society, vol. 46 (2010–11).

22 Spinks, op. cit., p. 61.

23 Ibid., pp. 214–15.

24 Reference should also be made to the earlier seminal document *Music and Liturgy*, trans. Paul Inwood (Washington: Pastoral Press, 1992), which reflected the work of the France-based group Universa Laus before and after Vatican II, which it much influenced.

25 Irmgard Pahl, 'Music and the liturgical celebration', *Studia Liturgica* 28:1 (1998), 1–13, translated from the German by Robert J. Daly, SJ.

26 Don E. Saliers, 'The integrity of sung prayer', *Worship* 55:4 (1981), pp. 290ff. However, in later works, such as *Music and Theology* (Nashville: Abingdon Press, 2007), he takes a wider theological sweep.

27 John D. Witvliet, 'The virtue of liturgical discernment', in Charlotte Kroeker (ed.), *Music in Christian Worship* (Collegeville: Liturgical Press, 2005), pp. 92–5.

28 *Annual of the Church Service Society*, vols 31 (May 1961) and 35 (May 1965).

29 A WCC-sponsored gathering at Ditchingham, England, in 1994 was convened to begin a parallel exploration through the medium of liturgy of the themes being pursued in theological dialogue at the time. See T. F. Best and D. Heller (eds), *So We Believe, So We Pray: Towards Koinonia in Worship,* Faith and Order Paper 171 (Geneva: WCC Publications, 1995).

30 *Music in Catholic Worship*, (American) Bishops' Committee on the Liturgy (1972). In 2007, the Bishops returned to the task with *Sing to the Lord: Music in Divine Worship*.

31 This objection was particularly expressed in the Snowbird Statement, the result of two gatherings in North America of Roman Catholic theologians and church musicians, published in 1995.

32 Erik Routley, *Church Music and Theology* (London: SCM Press, 1959); *Church Music and the Christian Faith* (London: Collins, 1980).
33 H. Ridderbos, *Paul: An Outline of His Theology* (London: SPCK, 1977), p. 362.
34 J. Gros, H. Meyer and W. G. Rusch, *Growth in Agreement II: Reports and Agreed Statements of Ecumenical Conversations on a World Level, 1982–1998*, Faith and Order Paper 187 (Geneva: WCC, 2000), p. 450.
35 Don E. Saliers, *Music and Theology* (Nashville: Abingdon Press, 2007), p. 70.
36 Nathan D. Mitchell, 'The amen corner', *Worship* 78:1 (2004), p. 61.
37 This can be found in *Church Hymnary* 4, no. 533.
38 Another example is the Korean melody to 'God who made the earth' (*Church Hymnary* 4, no. 228).
39 *Common Ground: A Hymnbook for All the Churches* (Edinburgh: Saint Andrew Press, 1998), no. 55.
40 *The English Hymnal* (1906).
41 Particularly John N. Collins, *Diakonia: Re-Interpreting the Ancient Sources* (Oxford: Oxford University Press, 1990).